John Peisley
Australian Bushranger

By Julie Kincade

Copyright © Julie Kincade. All rights reserved. No part of this book may be reproduced, stored in a retrieval system, or transmitted in any form or by any means, electronic, mechanical, photocopying, recording, or otherwise, without the prior written permission of the Copyright owner.

ISBN 978-0-6481599-3-3
Published 2024

 A catalogue record for this work is available from the National Library of Australia

DISCLAIMER

Every effort has been made to ensure that information in this book is accurate, including where possible sourcing information from documents "of the day" such as published obituaries, newspaper articles, wills, and criminal records. Intrinsic to this book is the use of digitised versions of historic newspapers, however not all newspapers have been digitised and not all search indexes are complete, therefore not all information may be available online or offline. It is always possible that mistakes can occur, things change, and improvements can be made, however, no responsibility can be accepted for any loss, injury or inconvenience sustained by any person using this book or by any business, organisation or individual featured in this book.

Contents

Goodbye Gentlemen	5
About Peisley	7
Far from the tree	11
A horse affair	33
Old Bathurst Gaol	39
Off for a nobbler	45
Cockatoo Island	49
Lambing Flat Riots	61
On the run	65
Fogg's Hut	77
Cohorts	95
The Invisible Prince	101
Benyon	111
Capture	121
Trial	131
Hanged man	139
Reaction	143
Aftermath	149
Epitaph	153
Other info	155
Index	163

The true story of

John Peisley
Australian Bushranger

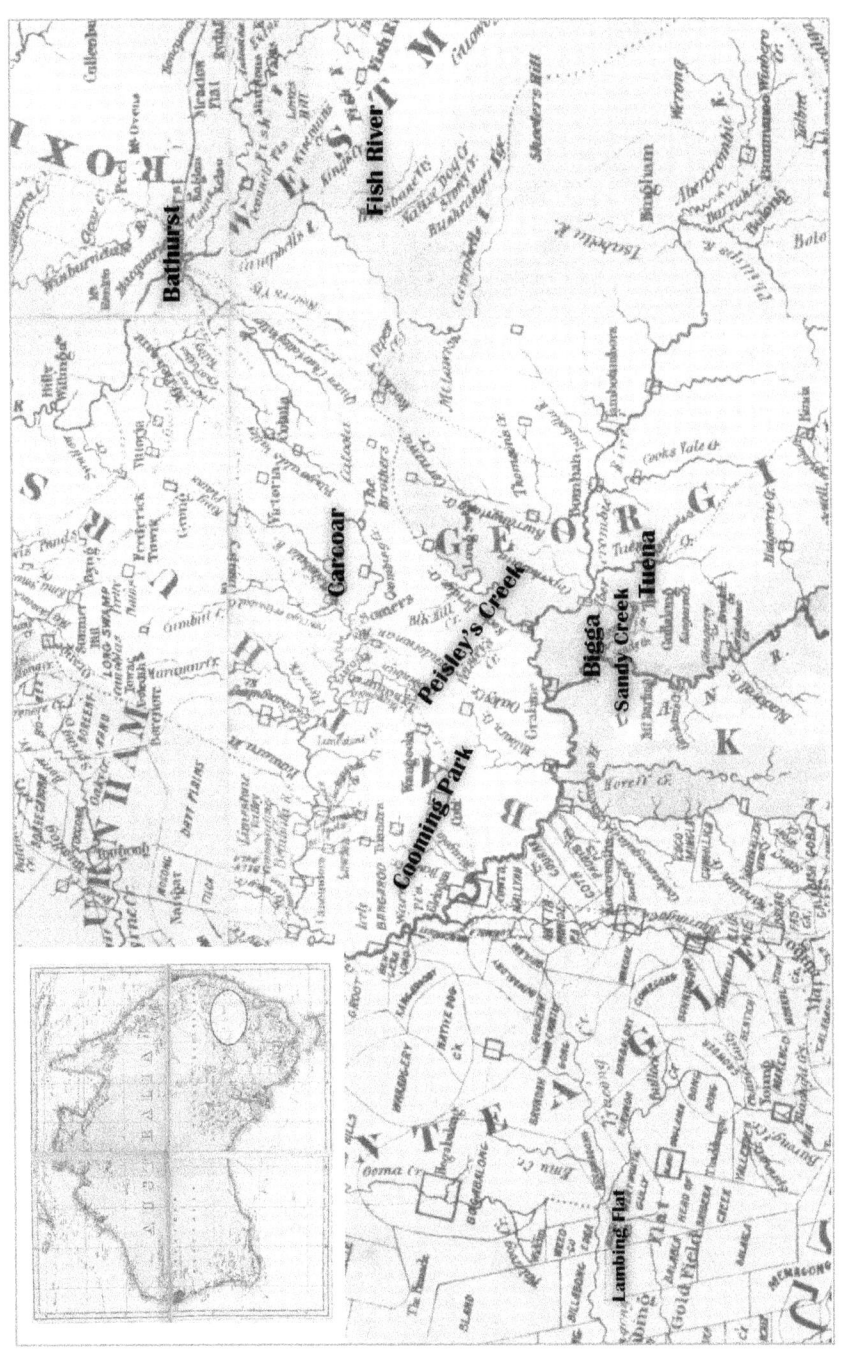

Reuss & Browne's map of New South Wales 1860

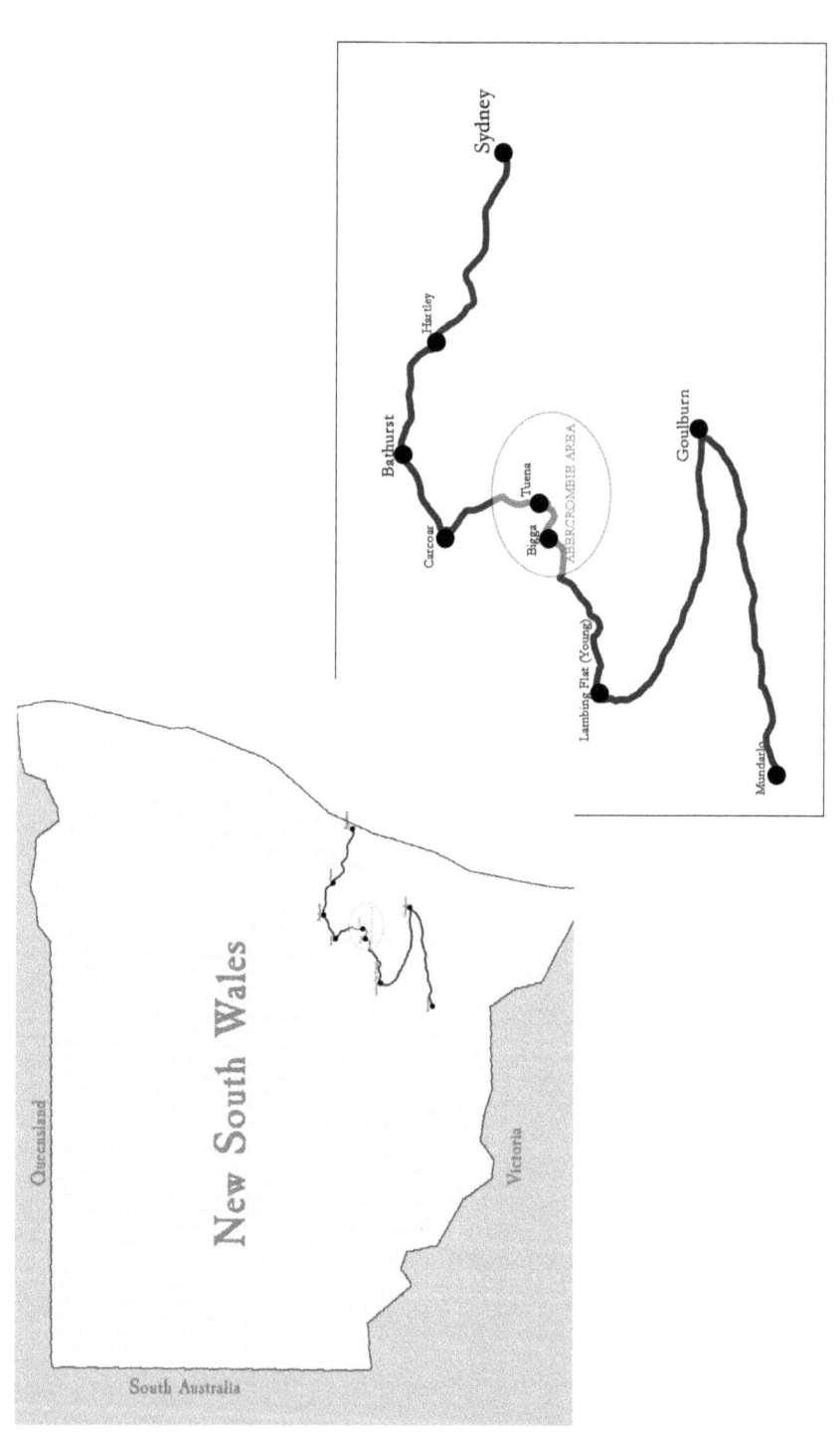

Foreword

As any family historian knows, the lives of ancestors are often chronicled around dramas - those of war, of changing political and economic conditions. It doesn't matter what your descension is – European, Indigenous, Asian or Middle Eastern etc, to trace ancestry, the timeline usually follows dramatic world events that are now the subject of countless studies. Then we trace according to local events. Often those are found in family stories, in newspapers and other local records.

I have many rogues in my family tree – lots of transported convicts, plenty that got themselves into weird situations. I also have heroes encompassing just about every civil conflict … WWI & WWII, the Boer War, the German Revolution and Franco-Prussian War, even a few that were at the Eureka Rebellion. There are many refugees as well.

John Peisley though is Australian born – my 2x great uncle. There are no war stories here. No accounts of amazing industry or heroics. And yet, by a country mile, his appearance dwarfs all others in prevalence. As an Australian Bushranger, today he's not widely known. His name certainly isn't the first to spring up when our historical rebels enter the discussion. However, his story is right up there in terms of drama.

Hopefully this book will reveal – if not at least document in some way – his extraordinary life, how it was shaped by others and how he coped with the many dramas that played out in colonial Australia. And I must say, I'm proud to place him in my family tree.

April 1862

Thursday, 2 pm

Between three and four o'clock this morning several of the inhabitants of Bathurst experienced a slight shock of an earthquake; but as far as I can learn, no damage has been done.

The weather at present is threatening, with heavy black clouds towards south-east.

— The Sydney Morning Herald,
Friday 25 April 1862, page 4

Goodbye Gentlemen

In 1862, John Peisley was found guilty of the wilful murder of William Benyon. Sentenced to death, on the morning of Friday 26 April 1862, John Peisley was taken from his cell at the Bathurst Gaol and led to the gallows within its precinct. Around fifty people had gathered to watch him hang by the neck until dead.

His conduct up to the point of meeting his death was described as highly commendable with the Reverend attending him finding him exceedingly apt and attentive to his instructions. His demeanour did not show the hardened, careless spirit known as "the game" - a term widely used to describe the activities of bushrangers. He was described as having manifested the "coolness and determination of a man with the strongest nerve."

The day prior, his sister Elizabeth visited him at the gaol. He was allowed to speak freely with her, but then he told her not to come again. In the morning his brother Benjamin, also visited during which he offered some advice, hoping his plight would prove a warning to him and others.

At exactly at nine o'clock, wearing chains around his ankles and hands, he was taken to the scaffold while a portion of the funeral service was read. On reaching the foot of the gallows, he knelt in prayer with the clergymen.

He then shook hands with the clergy and turned to the crowd. In his dying statement he talked of his demise, stating that if any man were guilty of committing such a murder as was represented by the evidence given at his trial, he would justly deserve to die. He hoped that God would forgive all his enemies; he forgave them freely, and fully. He concluded by saying "Goodbye gentlemen, and God bless you."

The fatal rope was then adjusted and a white cap was placed over his head. By a signal from the Acting-Sheriff, the drop fell and John Peisley was sent to eternity.

He did not suffer much nor long. After hanging the usual time, his body was cut down and placed in a coffin to be conveyed to his final resting place. He was twenty eight years old.

About Peisley

No account of Australian history is complete without some reference to our bushrangers – the men (and women) who ran rampant on our roads and through towns throughout the nineteenth century. Whether they appeal to our love of rebels, or they show how tough life was in this new colonial landscape, there is nothing generic in their personal histories. Nothing that we can pin down to definitively say, this person would become a bushranger. They came from all walks of life.

There are the "celebrity" bushrangers such as Ned Kelly, Ben Hall and Frank Gardiner. Then there are perhaps our "B" list bushrangers such as Captain Moonlight (Andrew Scott), Mad Dog Morgan (Daniel Morgan) and Captain Thunderbolt (Fred Ward) as well as a long list of their partners in crime such as John Vane, Harry Power, Dan Kelly and John Dunn. The list goes on. If your claim to fame was highway robbery and your preferred mode de vie was being constantly on the run from the law, then you would probably be on the list.

John Peisley was certainly one of these, and for all intents, he remained there for most of his life. He always gets a mention in any account written about Frank Gardiner – they were mates and Peisley got him into trouble. Sometimes he factors in the Ben Hall story – he was a bushranger around the same time. He may have inspired Ned Kelly, but that's stretching his fame.

However, Peisley's full story is not widely known. He certainly hasn't found his glory in a plethora a books and films. He does have his own page on Wikipedia. But in his day - in the 1860s - his antics made the newspapers on almost a daily basis. Many of those antics attributed to Peisley, possibly incorrectly.

This book will attempt to take a deep dive into Peisley's history, the circumstances surrounding his upbringing, the events that led to his death and hopefully everything in between. What made him become a bushranger? What made him different? Was he treated fairly? Was his death necessary or even warranted?

How did he start?

Exactly how long John Peisley had been in the Abercrombie district of New South Wales, to the west of the Blue Mountains, is unknown. What is known is that he was born in 1834 but there doesn't appear to be a birth record for him in the New South Wales official records.

Some research suggests that Peisley was born in Penrith and spent his first fifteen years there – certainly his grandparents lived in Penrith at the time. Others say that Peisley and his siblings were all born and raised in the Carcoar area, just south west of Bathurst, and possibly at Cooming Park, a pastoral estate where his father worked.

However, the most credible evidence is that he spent his first years at his grandparents farm in the apples district near Penrith, then went to live with his parents at age ten or eleven around 1845. What is certain is that after an accusation made by the Peisley's neighbour and owner of Cooming Park, Thomas Icely, the following year, his father was sent to gaol at Cockatoo Island and then his mother went to live with another man at Bathurst. So, by age fourteen or fifteen, John Peisley was alone in the bush.

After losing their father to gaol in Sydney and their mother to Bathurst, the Peisley children had to fend for themselves. It is possible the younger children were raised by their sister Elizabeth (junior), who in 1849 at age sixteen, married Owen Drady, a transported convict holding a ticket of leave, aged forty three. They lived in the Abercrombie bush.

Regardless of how long John Peisley had to become accustomed to the bush, it didn't take long for him to stray.

Far from the tree

In any investigation into John Peisley it is worth looking into his upbringing as it is obvious that his early development was to play a huge part in his life. John Peisley was the first son born of transported convicts Thomas Peisley and Elizabeth Clayton.

Thomas Peisley - father

His father Thomas hailed from Alderton in Northamptonshire, England. At that time he was known as Thomas Peasland. In July of 1819, Thomas and two others faced the Northampton Assizes on a charge of highway robbery, having held up and robbed a fellow on the King's

Highway near Alderton. For their crime, they were each sentenced to death - a penalty common for criminals in Britain in the day. Shortly thereafter, their sentences were reprieved "before the Judge left town." This didn't set them free, they were still incarcerated, however this was not the end of their travels.

In October 1819, Thomas Peisley and his robbing cohorts were resident on a ship called the "Bellerophon", infamous for being the vessel upon which Napoleon had surrendered. After it was decommissioned as a Naval vessel and following an extensive refit, the sixteen hundred ton Bellerophon spent her last days housing upwards of four hundred and thirty British prisoners. While there were intentions to sail the Bellerophon to New South Wales as part of the convict transports, she was eventually found not seaworthy so stayed put. The Bellerophon was by no means a luxury place to be.

Conditions on the prison hulks were purposefully substandard. The inmates were fed a limited diet as set out in the Parliamentary "Hulk Act" which stipulated they received little other than bread, any coarse or inferior food, water and some beer. Consequently, many convicts became malnourished and it is estimated that up to a third died as a result, especially as sanitation on the hulks was, even by the lowest of modern standards, non-existent and disease such as cholera, dysentery and typhus ran rampant. Daily life usually consisted of hard labour on the docks or nearby fields, unpaid, often brutally overseen. In short, if you evaded execution by confinement to a prison hulk, you were lucky. If you survived the conditions on the hulk, you were even luckier. So in this respect Thomas Peisley was luckier than some.

In April 1820, nearly a full year after his conviction, Thomas Peisley, still in chains, was boarded onto the ship Agamemnon - a five hundred and forty two ton sailing ship - along with one hundred and seventy eight other male prisoners and at the beginning of May, the Agamemnon set sail for Australia via Rio. The prisoners disembarked at Port Jackson in Sydney Harbour in September 1820, marking nearly five months at sea. It was in Sydney that Thomas was to serve the remainder of his seven year sentence.

Soon after arrival Thomas was consigned to work for an agriculturalist and produce dealer in Sydney. He got into some trouble when he united with a rebel group of striking workers resulting in two years being added to his sentence. He was transported to Newcastle, eventually ending up working for Reverend Samuel Marsden, a missionary and sheep farmer, however even this didn't keep him on the right side of the law.

In October 1824, while still attached to Marsden's "clearing gang", Thomas was among a group of men charged with harbouring bushrangers and refusing to assist with their apprehension. Yes, even as early as 1824 the "colony" had bushrangers, and Thomas was obviously no stranger to them. For this crime he received twenty five lashes.

Looking at Thomas's history, it is not difficult to conclude that his son John Peisley learned his craft of crime early, or rather that he was never taught right from wrong. It's easy to believe that part of his wayward ways could be attributed to his early parental influences - Peisley's mother will be discussed later. The story of his father Thomas however, doesn't end there.

In December 1826, a full seven and half years after his initial conviction in England, Thomas Peisley was finally granted a Certificate of Freedom in Australia. With this in hand he could have returned to England, however as most freed convicts found, transportation to Australia did not include a return ticket. Travel to England in the 1820s was an expensive proposition and more than likely, having spent sentences in servitude, without compensation beyond food and shelter, travel to such a degree would have been beyond any convict's means. The idea of transportation was of course to punish rather than reform criminals, and Thomas probably faced his freedom with nothing more than the shirt on his back, and a stretch of over twenty thousand kilometres to home.

The years following his emancipation are a little unclear and he appears to have stayed on the straight and narrow, or at least he disappeared from the news reports. However, with freedom in hand, he finally had some good fortune by way of family.

Firstly, at age thirty three, he married Elizabeth Clayton in January 1830. Over the coming years the couple had several children including Sarah (born 1830), Elizabeth (born 1832), John (born 1834), Benjamin (born 1838), Matthew (born 1843), Mary (born 1844) and William (born 1846). There is some evidence of another son, Thomas Francis (born 1844), but the official records do not support this - he is likely a cousin. While no official records of the children's birth were found, they all appear to have been born (or registered) either at Carcoar in western New South Wales, or at Penrith where their grandparents lived. Following Thomas Peasland's marriage to

Elizabeth, he became known as Thomas Peisley, with all the children born Peisley.

The family's activities over the sixteen year period from 1830 to 1846 one can only guess. It is known that Thomas did work for Thomas Icely, a wealthy squatter on a twenty six thousand acre pastoral run known as Cooming Park, to the south of Carcoar. History has written that Icely was granted the "use" of sixty two male convicts to help develop Cooming Park, including mustering and building. In a census published in 1837, of the near fifteen hundred adult inhabitants of the County of Bathurst, which encompassed Carcoar, sixty percent of them were convicts, with the Colonial Government providing a set ration of food, most likely funded from land sales and leases to the pastoralists. To some degree, the Government services required in these new developing districts such as hospitals, schools, policing, building roads, water etcetera, indicate that revenue generated from pastoral leasing in these areas was unlikely to have filled the Colonial coffers, however it did sustain a lot of people who otherwise may have found themselves starving, destitute or dead.

What is known of Thomas Peisley though, is that in this period he made several applications for land leases around the Carcoar area. In 1837 he made applications for six parcels of land in the areas bordering Rocky Bridge Creek. These applications were denied and the land left vacant. In correspondence with the Colonial Treasurer, he was advised the land was advertised for sale, not lease, so he again applied in 1838, however it appears the application was made too late, and the land was sold to another person. The following year, he made application to purchase one hundred acres at Neville, but this too was refused.

At some point over the following ten years, Thomas Peisley settled his family on land near Carcoar, the position of which is best determined to be between Rocky Bridge Creek and Peisley's Creek, near the mouth of the Abercrombie River, on land then bordering Cooming Park. As no official lease can be found in the land register of the day, it is assumed their occupation wasn't strictly legal, however this wasn't uncommon among the convicts in the area.

For a time, it appeared that life was reasonably normal – the Peisley's ran a few hundred head of cattle, the children were often sent to Penrith, the home of Elizabeth Peisley's parents, where they received some form of education. Then it all came to an abrupt halt.

The Durham Pet Bull

This story is worth repeating here, not necessarily about John Peisley directly however it can explain how John was essentially left fatherless at the tender age of just 15. One can only theorise the impact this would have on a young boy's life.

In February of 1848, Thomas Peisley faced court on a charge of stealing a bull belonging to his neighbour, Thomas Icely of Cooming Park. This was not a civil case – an argument between Icely and Thomas Peisley which would have been rectified by a settlement between the two. Instead Peisley was being tried as a criminal – his crime of theft was against the Crown and thus carried the potential for gaol time.

As the day long court case commenced, Icely was the first to give evidence. He said that in 1841 he imported from England two valuable animals. One was a Devonshire cow. The other was a Durham bull that he paid two hundred guineas for. He went on to say that a few years later, the cow had a bull calf, which at two months of age was branded by Icely's farm superintendent. The brand was a TI on the shoulder and near the rump, and a small T on the cheek. He claimed the face brand was to distinguish cattle that were of a valuable and improved breed.

The calf and it's mother were then turned out into a paddock Icely kept "expressly for cattle of a superior description."

When the calf was seven months old (late 1844) and fully weaned, it was moved into another paddock kept "expressly for de-pasturing" high class cattle. Then after a few further months it was turned out into a run. In these days there were no fences separating paddocks, only stockmen and shepherds kept the herds in check.

Nearly two years had passed when, in late 1846, Icely's superintendent sent him a letter telling him the animal was missing. Icely was in Sydney at the time. On his return to Cooming Park a few weeks later, the animal had still not been located.

Another year passed. Icely then claimed that he saw the animal in his own stockyard, where it had been bought by his own people. He said another brand had been placed on the bull – a TP over a TP – which was the brand used by Thomas Peisley. Icely said he asked for the brand areas to be shaved, stating that he found beneath the remains of his own brand, albeit imperfect (which he blamed on the lack of skill of his branding man.)

He then swore positively that without any brand whatsoever, he would at any time have been able to pick out the bull from a hundred or even a thousand animals of a similar description. He described in some detail the breed being so very superior, and that he himself had travelled with the dam and sire on the ship from England to Australia some five years earlier and reiterated the great expense he had incurred to have them in his herd.

His testimony attempted to hit the emotional heartstrings of the jury when he stated that the animal had become a "pet" with him, and he "had taken more notice of it than of any other on his estate." Bear in mind Icely spent most of his time in Sydney and the bull had been missing for more than a year.

At the time of the court case, the bull was being held in the yards at the Courthouse, with Icely claiming that he "most positively and distinctly" believed it was the bull he had described, and his property, that he could "not by any possibility be mistaken."

Continuing with testimony, the court was then told that when the bull turned up in Icely's stockyard, Thomas Peisley went to Cooming Park and threatened to sue Icely for the return of the bull.

It was then time for Icely's stockmen to take the witness stand. One of his superintendents agreed with all Icely had said, adding that the bull had apparently been sent from Icely's estate to the Carcoar pound. The stockman who drove it to the pound swore that he did so by order of the superintendent (which was later denied by the said superintendent who claimed he was absent from the estate and could not have possibly given such an order.)

The bull had been at the Carcoar pound for about six days when Thomas Peisley called in and told the pound keeper the bull was his property. He was told the pound fee was £5 to which Peisley said he would pay only five shillings being the pound keeper's fee and that the pound keeper should claim the rest from the stockman who took the bull to the pound. On these terms the bull was delivered over to Peisley. The pound keeper had asked Peisley why he had not before branded the bull and was told that it had gone astray which prevented him from doing so, but he would forthwith do so, and which, from the testimony of other witnesses, it appeared he did.

Testimony from some of the other witnesses described the fact that Peisley's run joined the Cooming Park run and that cattle from the two runs frequently intermixed. It was noted that as Icely's imported Durham bull was allowed to go at large in the neighbourhood of the Peisley run and the cattle therein, it was probable Peisley may have become possessed of a bull calf resembling the one claimed by Icely. However, it was the evidence given by three witnesses, who swore that the animal in dispute bore the brands, or portions of the brands, of Icely, that held the most weight in all the heard testimony.

During the trial, Peisley's Counsel, Arthur Holroyd, frequently objected to the evidence attempted to be elicited by the Attorney-General, but the Judge in almost every case overturned these objections, to the degree that Holroyd requested the Judge take notes of his objections, in order that they might be brought under the consideration of the full Court.

In his defence Peisley presented two witnesses, both stockmen that had both been in the service of Icely for several years. The first witness stated he saw the birth of Icely's bull-calf dropped by the Devon cow in January 1844 and that shortly after it had been calved, at about two months old, it was branded very plainly and distinctly. He had seen the animal frequently from the time it was branded until he left Icely's employ in January 1846, at which time he said the brands were very plain and distinct. Another defence witness stated that he was present at the branding of the calf dropped by the Devon cow, that the brands were put on very clearly and that he had seen the calf almost daily until he quit Icely's employ in April 1846. Holroyd then asked for this witness to be allowed to inspect the bull being held at the Courthouse, which he did. On his return to the Court, the witness stated that he could not see any distinct traces of the Icely brand on the spots where they should be - there were some marks, but in his opinion they were not brand marks.

Following this, both sides of the case, the Crown and Peisley's defence, rested. It took the Judge nearly two hours to sum up the case to the Jury, who then retired to reach their verdict. After an absence of about five minutes the Jury returned with a verdict of guilty of cattle stealing, with Peisley remanded overnight for sentencing. It was written in the press that the case excited very considerable interest, and noted how the courtroom was filled with "a greater number of wealthy stockholders than we have witnessed for a long time past."

The following day, the Judge sentenced Thomas Peisley to seven years hard labour on the public roads meaning he was to serve his sentence in gaol.

From Bathurst, in early March 1848 he was transported to Darlinghurst Gaol, some two hundred kilometres east. Then six months later he was moved to the prison at Cockatoo Island in Sydney Harbour, where he was to remain. There was no consideration of the impact this would have on his family.

Thomas Peisley was granted a ticket of leave in September 1851 having served three years of his sentence. He was released from Cockatoo with a condition that he remain in the district of Yass. From here is it unknown what happened to him, including when or where he finally died. He doesn't appear on any list of absconders from the Yass district in the future years, so it is assumed that he remained there.

Thomas's story provides echoes into the future life of his son John. Kinship with bushrangers – yes. Running foul of wealthy landowners and people of influence – indeed. Court cases and incarceration at Cockatoo Island – absolutely. All things that would become the familiar environment for John Peisley.

So what did happen to the family of Thomas Peisley? His wife and his children? Because of his conviction, the family had to immediately forfeit and surrender their cattle to the government, some five hundred head. The Government sold them at auction six weeks later and in effect this left the Peisley family destitute.

CATTLE, AT CARCOAR.

MR. STEWART has received instructions to sell by auction, at his Rooms, in York-street, on

WEDNESDAY, MAY 3RD,

CERTAIN CATTLE, said to muster about

500 HEAD,

Now running in the district of Carcoar, and forfeit to

THE CROWN,

By the conviction of Thomas Peisley of felony.

Also,

At the same time and place, there will be sold another lot of cattle said to muster about

100 HEAD,

forfeit to the Crown by the conviction of R. Duggan for felony.

Further particulars in future advertisements.

6392

The Sydney Morning Herald, 13 April 1848, page 4

Elizabeth Peisley - mother

Abruptly and perhaps unfairly, following the incarceration of her husband Thomas, John Peisley's mother Elizabeth was suddenly left in the middle of nowhere, without a means and with several small children to care for. What became of her?

Elizabeth Peisley was born in 1812, the daughter of Sarah Green and Matthew Clayton. Elizabeth never knew her father. Her mother was a house servant in London when she was arrested for stealing a watch and shawl from a lodger staying in the house. Her crime was listed as a "breach of trust" and for that she was sentenced to death. She was twenty three years old.

Following her trial, Sarah Green spent nine months in gaol awaiting her execution. Albeit rare for females, at some point she may have been removed to a prison hulk. What is known is that while in prison, Sarah became pregnant. She started calling herself Sarah Clayton and named her "husband" as Matthew Clayton, a ship's carpenter, however no official marriage record has been located.

While death was a heavy sentence for a crime not even described as petty theft, like Thomas Peisley, Sarah got a reprieve when, along with other female convicts, she boarded the ship "Mistral" and set sail to Australia in June 1812 as a transported convict. Her term to serve was life imprisonment. Somewhere near Indonesia, aboard the Mistral, Sarah gave birth to a daughter, Elizabeth Clayton, before finally arriving in Sydney in October 1812. Upon arrival in Australia, the newborn Elizabeth was also classed as a convict, despite never having committed a crime. She was to serve her years in Australia with the same sentence as her mother - life imprisonment.

Convict females arriving in the colony were usually sent out to work as domestic servants. In the 1824 census Sarah was living in the agricultural area of Windsor, at a farm near Penrith. In 1828 she was again listed in Penrith as married to another former convict, Matthew Buckley. Sarah eventually received her freedom via a conditional pardon in 1818, however she remained in Penrith, living as Sarah Buckley for the rest of her days. She died at the Sydney Benevolent Asylum in 1844.

Her daughter Elizabeth was also resident at the Penrith farm in 1828, with her mother and stepfather. Two years later Elizabeth married Thomas Peisley when she was just eighteen years old.

Thomas was nearly twice her age, but they set about having their family. What is known is that Elizabeth and the children spent some time at Penrith, as it was here that she gave birth to son Matthew in 1843. However, by the time of Thomas' incarceration in 1848, she was living at the farm near Carcoar.

When her husband Thomas was sent to Cockatoo Island for stealing the Icely bull, Elizabeth was left destitute.

That month she penned a lengthy letter to the press pleading for clemency:

April 1848

> To the Editor of the Sydney Morning Herald. Gentlemen, As a lonely and desolate woman, deprived by the interference of the law of the aid and support of a husband, and unacquainted

with the means of obtaining redress by an appeal to law, and unable through poverty to do so, I now take the liberty of soliciting a space in the columns of your very widely circulated journal, to present to the public notice a plain and simple statement of fact connected with the conviction of my husband, in the fond hope that it may meet the eyes either of His Excellency the Governor or some of the humane and influential members of the legal profession, and induce them to afford a due consideration to the case, and obtain for my husband not any extension of clemency, not any act of mercy, but to afford to an innocent man that justice to which he is entitled.

The case is simply as follows:

—In the month of January 1846, my husband, Thomas Peisley, lost a young bull of the Durham breed, unbranded, which had been saved for a man named Thomas Pye, who had requested my husband to preserve one for him. After a long and fruitless search for the animal, my husband enquired of the pound keeper at Carcoar, whether a beast of the description had been ever noticed by him, or whether such an one had ever been sold from thence. The pound keeper replied that one answering exactly to the description given was then in the pound, having been impounded from Mr Icely's, by John Kater, the overseer of Mr Icely.

My husband recognised the beast as being his lost property, and on being informed by the pound keeper that £5 damages had been laid, he declined paying anything but the poundage, saying that the overseer might sue him for the damage if he liked, for the bull was as good as any of Mr Icely's. He then released the bull, took it home, and branded it.

In some ten or twelve months afterwards, my husband was informed that John Kater, the same overseer for Mr Icely, had taken the same bull, another bull, and other cattle, sending the other bull and other cattle to the pound, but detaining the bull before alluded to.

My husband, on ascertaining that such was really the case, went himself to Kater and demanded by what authority he detained his (my husband's) beast. Kater replied that he detained it because Mr Icely had lost a bull of the same description, and he suspected this to be the bull lost. My husband then enquired whether Mr Icely's bull was branded, to which Kater replied in the affirmative, stating that it was branded TI on the hip and shoulder. My husband then told him that this bull could not be Mr Icely's, as there was no other brand upon it but his own. Kater replied that he did not care, but that he would detain the beast until the arrival of Mr Icely.

My husband told him that it was optional with him whether he would leave it or not, but he left it until Mr Icely's arrival, a period of about eight weeks. On Mr Icely's arrival my husband, instead of obtaining his beast, was apprehended upon a warrant procured by Mr Icely from his brother-in-law, Mr Rotheray, upon Mr Icely's farm, whither he had gone for the purpose of claiming his property. He was subsequently committed upon a charge of cattle stealing. My husband was brought to trial at the Bathurst Assizes, February 1848, on which occasion the following is an abstract of the evidence adduced:

— Mr Icely swore to the beast, and said that it was branded TI on the shoulder. John Kater swore to the same effect. Mr Rotheray swore to the same effect. C Spinks, the Carcoar pound keeper, swore to it being branded in the manner described by Messrs Icely and Rotheray, though the Gazette was produced in Court in which this identical witness had published the same beast as unbranded!

Mark Mills, Mr Icely's stockman, deposed: That he himself brought in the bull in question, and took it to the pound by the order of John Kater, as a strange and unbranded beast, and laid thereon the damages of £5. He also swore to having seen Mr Icely's bull two days previous to impounding the bull in question.

James Williams, ticket-of-leave holder, deposed: That he was herdsman to Mr Icely before Mills; that he roped and threw Mr Icely's calf, and that Mr J Kinchela branded it. He had seen the calf scores of times since, and saw Mr Icely's brand upon it; the last time he saw the calf it was eighteen months old, he then saw the brand quite plain. The witness was then sent from the box by the Attorney-General, and desired to examine the bull in question.

On his return, the Attorney-General enquired whether the bull was branded? He replied that it was branded TP—TP. The Attorney-General enquired what other brand was on it? The witness replied—none. The Attorney-General enquired what brand was on the shoulder? The witness answered—No brand, nor any brand whatever on the cheek.

John Mowat: Was sixteen years in the service of Mr Icely; was overseer over all his stock; in January 1846, he was leaving Mr Icely's service, and had to muster all his stock. At this muster he mustered Mr Icely's bull, which was plainly branded TI hip and shoulder.

Such was the evidence upon which my husband was found guilty, and sentenced to be worked upon the roads for seven years. I should here remark that upwards of two hundred individuals examined the bull during the course of the trial, none of whom could discern Mr Icely's or any other brand than my husband's thereon. As my husband was unable to afford to keep servants in his employment, and compelled therefore to look after his farm himself, he had no witnesses to adduce in his behalf. But the case, such as it is, is now submitted to the notice of the public.

I submit it to their notice without comment, leaving it to themselves to draw the inference, whether justice has been done or not. I, however, humbly trust that my appeal to public sympathy may not be vain, and that the God of the afflicted will raise up for me and mine such friends as may support my humble claim for, and obtain for my oppressed husband that justice which a British subject is entitled to demand from the laws of his country. - Elizabeth Peisley, Little Forest, Carcoar, April 4th, 1848.

— The Sydney Morning Herald,
18 April 1848, page 1

There are three things to be said about this letter. Firstly, it was to no avail - Thomas was sent to Cockatoo Island and she was left to fend for herself and her children. Secondly, the wording appears to be from someone reasonably well educated, and lastly the letter was considered important enough for it to be published in full, prominently on the front page of a major Australian newspaper.

While Elizabeth's plight fell on deaf ears, the repercussions were wide ranging. The government wasted no time in confiscating their cattle. Despite having lived on their land possibly since at least the mid 1830s, the authorities were also keen to have the family removed, apparently thinking it was conscionable to leave a woman with her children abandoned in the bush.

Shortly after Thomas's incarceration, Elizabeth Peisley took up with a man of speculative origins - George Wilson, known locally as "Scotchy", likely as he hailed from Scotland. In one account of her movements after Thomas's incarceration she was described as having "absconded" with Scotchy, with the following summation: "In fact, modesty and virtue seem to have been altogether ignored in the family." This perhaps cruel description appears completely ignorant of the plight of women in the 1800s who were for all intents left destitute when husbands left of their free will or in chains, remembering that at this time, women had no rights. This is especially true for married women who, in the eyes of the law, gave up their entire identities upon marriage. They became "femme covert" – unable to own property, unable to borrow money, unable to enter into contracts, being merely a chattel owned by the husband, and yet still responsible for everything the husband did, even if he was absent.

In Elizabeth Peisley's situation, there was obviously little to no sympathy offered to a mother with children, and in the eyes of the law, nothing that could be done anyway.

George Wilson and Elizabeth do not appear to have married, and she remained by law married to Thomas despite his incarceration. However, Elizabeth went on to have four more children with Wilson, the last of which bought Elizabeth to her death following complications with the birth in 1856 at Bathurst. She was forty four years old. Her death certificate neglects to mention the children she bore with Thomas Peisley or her marital status, and her death being recorded as Elizabeth Wilson.

Of the children, the two eldest daughters married around the time of Thomas's incarceration, both at the age of sixteen. This left Elizabeth with at least five children under the age of fifteen, the youngest at just two years old. One of the children remained in Penrith with the grandparents and it is believed that the two older married daughters looked after the others.

John Peisley was around fourteen or fifteen years old – old enough to fend for himself and be useful but possibly too young to know the difference between right and wrong. With an impressionable young mind, and many bad examples to follow, it is not surprising that life went awry. His next ten or so years were filled with the only common theme in his life – gaol. Apart from the police lockup at Carcoar, his first real taste of incarceration was the old Bathurst Gaol.

A horse affair

John Peisley's first appearance in the press came shortly after his mother's departure. At this time it is believed that he was living with his sister Elizabeth and her husband Owen Drady on the Abercrombie River, south of Carcoar.

The charge was the first of a long line of accusations of horse stealing. In this case a man living at Grubbingbong near Carcoar, accused Peisley of stealing a horse he valued at £10. The man had been in search of Peisley for many months, tracking him as far south as Goulburn, however the law finally caught up with Peisley near Carcoar and they were applauded for their efforts:

September 1851

LACHLAN - Fortune favoured constable Robinson, who espied his man, a young native "gully-raker," of the name of Peisley, hard at work upon a flat. A reward of £3 has for some time been offered by Mr Thos McKell for Peisley's apprehension on a charge of horse-stealing. Perceiving Robinson's approach, he made a dash for the river, but was quickly overtaken and secured, and I understand is now safely deposited in Carcoar watch-house. Much praise is due to the Carcoar police for their conduct in this affair, and it is to be hoped that the well-disposed inhabitants of this region will give all the assistance in their power to expurgate the Abercrombie gullies of the marauders who have for a long time infested them, by conveying information to the police of their haunts.

— Bathurst Free Press and Mining Journal,
3 September 1851, page 3

Peisley faced court early the following year. Defended by solicitor Arthur Holroyd (who had also defended Thomas Peisley), Robinson and McKell were unable to convince the jury, and there was some doubt as to whether John Peisley was the right person, so John was found not guilty. However, he was immediately remanded to face a further charge of stealing horses belonging to Thomas Weavers at Mount Macquarie.

February 1852

> BATHURST ASSIZES - Some time last winter (witness could not fix the precise time) a person named Evans saw the prisoner Peisley driving seven horses which he said belonged to Mr Watts and further told witness that he was taking them to the Abercrombie. Among them were two horses very similar in many respects to those missed from the run of Mr Weaver. Evans told prisoner there was a warrant out against him for the stealing of these horses, when he denied their being the property of Weaver. Some doubt existed as to the horses being the same as those stolen from Weaver, on account of the brands being irregularly described by the two witnesses for the prosecution. The jury therefore, acquitted the prisoner of the charge without leaving the box.
>
> — Empire, 27 February 1852, page 3

As a petty criminal, horse stealing was John Peisley's preferred crime. In December 1852 at Bathurst he was again indicted for stealing two horses from a mail courier named Patrick Kurley.

Facing court in July 1854, this time Peisley was not so lucky. With the jury finding him guilty as charged, he was sentenced to five years on the roads or public works. He was admitted to Bathurst gaol, to be later transferred to Cockatoo Island in Sydney. By this time he was nineteen years old.

Escape from Weatherboard

While enroute from Bathurst to Cockatoo Island, Peisley and four other prisoners were housed overnight at the lockup known as "Weatherboard" near Hartley, a small township on the western side of the Blue Mountains. Overnight, the five managed to escape by lifting the floorboards of the building and wriggling the foundations enabling them to slip through the opening. It wasn't the first time prisoners had escaped from this lockup.

A report of the escape in the Australian Police Gazette included a description:

August 1854

> John Peisley, age 19, height 5 ft 9 in, hair light brown, eyes grey, first joint of third finger of left hand broken, crime horse stealing, sentence 5 years."
>
> — Australian Police Gazette No. 20, 1 August 1854, page 2

The report noted that all five men had their hair closely trimmed and wore prisoner clothing. It is imagined that in that attire their capture would have been somewhat straight forward, however Peisley remained on the run for nearly six weeks, finally being captured by the police back in the Abercrombie area. Along with Peisley, the police also seized two stolen horses he had with him. This time they kept him at Bathurst Gaol.

Old Bathurst Gaol

Many of the New South Wales bushrangers and criminals spent their sentences behind bars, it being the only penalty the courts could award, aside from death, as there was no such thing as good behaviour bonds. Being assigned to work in road gangs or on public works was how they spent their daytime hours, if they were lucky, or in irons consigned to cells if they were not so lucky.

Either way, if imprisonment was the only deterrent to crime available, what were the gaol conditions that were supposed to strike fear into the heads of those who broke the law?

In early 1861, the Hon William Windeyer, a member in the New South Wales Legislative Assembly, paid a visit to the Bathurst Gaol, during which he asked to have a casual look around. He was subsequently given the grand tour by the residing gaoler in charge.

What Windeyer found was a gaol in a state of considerable decay, stating that he found the gaol in "a filthy and neglected state, and swarming with vermin, that the turnkeys were lax and inattentive, and the prisoners' idle though sentenced to hard labour…" This description seems to fit most of the gaols of the day, especially those in country areas.

In the weeks following Windeyer's visit, the subject of the Bathurst Gaol's expenditure and management were raised for discussion in the Parliament. Windeyer made an impassioned speech about the deplorable state of the gaol. Not surprisingly, this drew attention from the local Bathurst authorities, obviously upset with Windeyer's summation. While they did not deny the state of the prison as being vermin ridden, they were particularly incensed by the accusation of mismanagement, leading one to write to the local press, denouncing Windeyer's claims.

What is obvious from the accounts of the Old Bathurst Gaol of the day is that prisons were the bottom of the pit in terms of the comfort and wellbeing of those incarcerated. Following the Windeyer appraisal however, there was a push to have the Bathurst Gaol overhauled and to remove what was then described as a "blot to the centre of their town".

The following year in July, the Department of Public Works invited tenders for alterations to the Bathurst Gaol, indicating the fact that while initially being regarded as damning, Windeyer's comments did result in some good.

Later in 1868, with the renovations complete, a further news article appraised the work done. This article relays to some degree the conditions prisoners such as John Peisley (and Jackie Bullfrog) endured in the lead up to their executions. Still, in the current day, these new supposedly more comfortable accommodations indicate the treatment faced by prisoners in the 1860s:

August 1868

> THE BATHURST GAOL - We paid a visit to the gaol on Wednesday last, and the notes we made will, no doubt, be of interest to the reader. Passing through the guard-room, we came to the corridor, which has been re-floored with hard timber throughout, and here we were shown the cells, which have undergone a complete transformation. Instead of boards, the floor of these compartments now consists of fourteen inches of concrete topped with a layer of cement three-quarters of an inch thick, and the walls which were lined with planks and afforded shelter for myriads of vermin, have been replaced with a facing of cement also three-quarters of an inch thick.
>
> This change necessitated some alteration being made in the sleeping arrangements, for while the prisoners could sleep on mattresses on the old wooden floor without inconvenience, the new floor of

concrete and cement would prove too cold in a building in which there are no fires to supply artificial heat. This difficulty was surmounted by a simple contrivance, suggested by Mr Forbes, which consists of two planks, each of a foot in width, placed in two detached pieces of quartering laid down at either end, in which a slot is cut to keep the boards in place. Upon this easily constructed bedstead the mattress is placed, and thus raised three or four inches above the ground to allow free ventilation beneath. These bed-boards are taken up every morning and replaced at night - the bedding and blankets being taken outside to be aired during the day. The cells throughout, are washed with lime, and present a scrupulously clean appearance.

The condemned cells in no way differ from the others, except in the presence of a heavy chain lying lengthways upon the ground and securely bolted to the walls, to which it is usual to hand-cuff one wrist of the culprit under sentence of death during the night, so that he may not have an opportunity of committing suicide, as one convict once very nearly succeeded in doing by hanging himself to the grated door, where he was found by the warders when life was nearly extinct.

The cells on the ground floor are only large enough to accommodate one prisoner, and they are used mostly for men who are committed for trial, or who are under remand. It is in the corridor that religious services are held, and instead of the male and female prisoners being placed, as formerly, in sight of each other, a movable screen is now stretched between them, at the side of which the officiating minister stands in sight of both divisions of his auditors, though they are unable to see anything beyond him. The middle floor is reached by a flight of broad stairs, and here we find the hospital and surgery. The former, however, offers far too little accommodation in the event of sickness, and some better provision is urgently required.

Rows of cells range along the sides of the building, and a railed gallery runs round to admit access to them. The compartments are of much larger dimensions than those on the ground floor, and are each used for the confinement at night of three or four of the prisoners sentenced to hard labour, to whose safe keeping this division of the gaol is set apart.

The upper floor is used for short-sentenced prisoners, and here is the school in which boys and youths receive instruction, and the cells in size and all other arrangements are similar to those on the middle floor.

Everywhere the prison is the pattern of cleanliness; lime and paint being used unsparingly on walls and doors, and brushes and dusters searching out every nook and cranny, where there is the slightest suspicion of any accumulating filth.

— The Sydney Morning Herald,
11 August 1868, page 6

Bathurst to Cockatoo

After the Weatherboard escape, John Peisley was held at the pre renovated Bathurst Gaol.

At a hearing in the Bathurst Circuit Court some months later, a judge ruled on the escape and ordered that Peisley spend one month in the Parramatta Gaol to commence at the end of his original sentence. In February 1855, Peisley finally arrived at Cockatoo Island.

Off for a nobbler

John Peisley was received at Cockatoo Island in Sydney on 14 February 1855. One of the other prisoners resident at Cockatoo when Peisley arrived was Frank Gardiner, another of Australia's most notorious bushrangers. They had something in common - they were both sent to Cockatoo Island for horse stealing, Gardiner arriving in April 1854 from Goulburn. Gardiner was then twenty four years old and Peisley twenty one years old. This meeting was to commence Peisley's long association with Frank Gardiner – more on that later.

In March 1857, just two years into his sentence, Peisley was transferred from Cockatoo Island back to Parramatta Gaol where he was required to serve one month relating to the escape from the Weatherboard lockup. Time served, at the end of April, he was discharged from Parramatta, but not empty handed - he left Parramatta Gaol with a ticket of leave. According to the National Library of Australia, a "Ticket of Leave allowed convicts to work for themselves provided they remained in a specified area, reported regularly to local authorities and attended divine worship every Sunday, if possible. They could not leave the colony." This is loosely what we would today call parole.

Peisley's ticket restricted him to remain within the Goulburn district, to the south west of New South Wales. He didn't. In fact he headed some two hundred kilometres north, to the east of the Blue Mountains, where his grandparents ran a fifty acre farm on the banks of the Nepean River at Evan, near Penrith. It was familiar ground and before long John Peisley was back in familiar work. With the ink barely dry on his Ticket of Leave, this was his next move:

December 1857

> HORSE STEALING - John Piesley (sic) was indicted for having, at Summerhill on the 1st July last, stolen three geldings and three colts, the property of one George Wylie. The prisoner pleaded not guilty, and was undefended. Mr Isaacs conducted the case for the prosecution.
>
> William Hobbs, chief constable of Windsor, being sworn, deposed: Met the prisoner in George street Windsor; asked him if he had not left some horses with Mr Seymour, the auctioneer, for sale; asked him how when, and where he had come by them, when he produced a receipt for two which he said he had

purchased; went with him to a stable where he had another animal, a mare, which he said he had ridden himself; prisoner gave his name as George Deason and said he had come from the Lachlan; witness feeling dissatisfied with the answers given, took prisoner with him to the auctioneers; while perusing the instructions given by prisoner to Seymour with regard to the sale of the horses, prisoner, who was then in custody of a constable, exclaimed, "Gentlemen, I'm off for a nobbler," and immediately ran away.

Witness followed, and after a smart chase came up with the prisoner, whom he secured and conveyed to the lock-up; prisoner had a knife in his hand when taken, but from his exhausted state was incapable of making use of it, if he desired to do so.

When taken before the magistrates at Windsor, prisoner gave his name as John Piesley (sic), and said he was a ticket-of-leave holder, and that being absent from his district, this was his reason for trying to escape from custody.

— Central Criminal Court, Empire,
9 December 1857, page 3

What is obvious from this is that John Peisley had no intention of leading a reformed life. There are conflicting news reports of this case, however not materially different - the result was the same.

Without retiring to consider their verdict, the jury immediately declared him guilty. He was then sentenced to a further five years to commence at the expiration of his previous sentence, meaning he had just turned two years of probation into seven years gaol and bought himself a ticket back to Cockatoo Island.

Cockatoo Island

At this point it is worth looking at what life was like for a prisoner serving time at Cockatoo Island. For all intents the Island's inmates were essentially employed as slave labour with punishment for their crimes to be dispensed in "public works", in this case, building a on an island located in the middle of Sydney Harbour. While convenient as a penal colony due to it's isolation, being surrounded by deep water, which was envisaged to prevent escape, but still accessible from the mainland settlement meaning prisoners could easily be supervised by the colonial administration. The design for Cockatoo appears to have been the establishment of a dock for receiving and storing goods shipped in from foreign ports. Labour for this construction came in the form of the prisoners housed therein.

At the start of 1857, there were over three hundred convicts held at Cockatoo Island. At that time, nearly all of them were employed in the construction of the dry dock, now known as Fitzroy Dock, with several other facilities such as granaries having already been established.

While the prisoners were held in dormitory style barracks, secondary areas, known as "the Cells", were also available to dispense further punishment for any misdemeanour among the prison population. These punishments were determined by the Island's Superintendent, Charles Ormsby, who had run the prison since 1841. The circumstances for those held for on-island punishment did not go unnoticed.

January 1857

COCKATOO ISLAND - THE CELLS

What terrible places of punishment! They are in the vicinity of the prisoners' barracks. Before entering what appears to the uninitiated, to be a large shed with a nice white flagged floor, you observe a sentinel with fixed bayonet and loaded musket marching to and fro in front of it. Inside you observe what you believe to be a number of gravestones - they are the doors lying horizontally; over the mouth of these dread places of punishment - beneath is the cell excavated out of the solid rook. These are eight or ten feet in depth, about seven feet long, and three feet wide; an excavation near the bottom looks like a seat or sleeping place.

High up in one of the side walls is a hole, intended no doubt for the admission of enough air and light to sustain life during the dread probationary entombment. The prisoner confined in these cells hears no voice or sound, except that of the person who lowers him down his daily supply of bread and water. The stoutest heart quails under this punishment, and indeed cases are not rare where entire physical prostration follows a confinement of three days, and the prisoner is so exhausted that he must, on the expiration of his punishment, be lifted out of his cell.

— Empire, 15 January 1857, page 5

In October 1857, Henry Parkes, then editor of the daily "Empire" and long-time critic of the activities at Cockatoo Island, reviewed the prison under Ormsby's rule:

October 1857

DISORDER ON COCKATOO ISLAND

The metropolitan prison of Cockatoo Island is an example in point enough to send a thrill of horror through every honest member of society.

— Empire, 2 October 1857, page 2

Parke's summation drew a lot of discussion, including name calling and blaming, however it was noticed by the highest voices in Sydney, including that of Charles Cowper, then the soon-to-be Colonial Secretary and Premier of New South Wales. One of Cowper's first actions was to call for an enquiry into the management of Cockatoo Island. A Board was established and in the first half of 1858, their comprehensive report was published.

April 1858

> THE COCKATOO ISLAND ENQUIRY
>
> The enquiry has been evidently a thorough one. They have not shirked any part of their wearisome and unpleasant duty. They have probed every accusation as far as they could possibly reach, and endeavoured honestly to get at the real truth.
>
> — South Australian Register, 13 April 1858, page 3

The Cabbage King

The Board's report into Charles Ormsby's supervision of the Island was damning. They found he often refused requests by guards and visitors for copies of the regulations of the prison, stating when asked, "Your duty is to obey orders." This led to officers neglecting their real duties or having them overruled.

The Board investigated an allegation that "prisoners have been arbitrarily and improperly sentenced to the cells for insolence (an undefined offence) to the Superintendent or overseers, and that the prisoners were treated in a manner to provoke insolence." An example was given of a Chinese prisoner's request for an interpreter being ignored, to the extent that he was kept in the cells until a visiting Magistrate arrived.

Ormsby was also criticised for not allowing inmates detained in the cells to attend religious services on Sundays. The charges then got worse as the character of Ormsby was revealed.

He was proved to have read prisoners' private letters aloud in the office, and made in a matter of jest, and that the contents of their letters to their friends were made known to fellow prisoners. He was also proved to have "appropriated" prisoner rations, such as maize, for his own use, later described as fed to the poultry and goats he kept on the Island, inferring that feeding animals was preferential to feeding prisoners. If a prisoner complained, he was sent to the cells.

It was also charged that Ormsby ordered maize to be boiled to the point where it became inedible, or meat purposefully undercooked, thus it became "refuse" and fed to his animals.

Being on the good side of Ormsby paid dividends, with allegations that he was partial to some, who then saw their freedom gained earlier than their sentence decreed. He was also accused of allowing the boats that should have only been used for official purposes, to be used by the security officers to do personal things such as go fishing. He often used the boats to entertain friends and family on overnight sails, making them unavailable for transporting people like chaplains and doctors to and from the Island. He also directed the boat crews to run personal errands to and from the mainland, again his personal use being prioritised over official use, and the accepted reason given for a boat's absence was that it was being "repaired".

There were many more charges, like using prisoners to hold boxing matches, however the Board then got to what they considered a serious infraction - that Ormsby was using the island and its convict labour to extensively grow produce that he then sold on the mainland for his own personal gain. The most prolific of these was cabbages, which Ormsby himself admitted that some thirty or forty thousand were grown at Cockatoo Island each year.

Apart from Ormsby, other breaches alleged to have occurred, involving the medical practitioners in the Island's hospital, were investigated, with some breaches leading to the death of the prisoner. The subordinate officers were also alleged to have regularly consumed alcohol, which was explicitly banned from the Island unless agreed by Ormsby.

On most of the charges investigated, Ormsby denied or refuted, often providing seemingly rational explanations, often supported by his close subordinates. Whether their compliance was coerced or not, the most telling statement on the activities on Cockatoo Island may be this:

March 1858

INQUIRY INTO THE MANAGEMENT OF COCKATOO ISLAND

No one systematically receives there the instruction which should fit him on his return to the society from which his crimes have banished, a better man, or better fitted for getting an honest livelihood. He returns a worse man in every respect than he went.

— Empire, 26 March 1858, page 3

No Escape?

According to Cockatoo Island records, there were a few escapes from the penal colony. Perhaps the most famous is that of Frederick Ward, another bushranger whose notoriety gained him the title "Captain Thunderbolt".

In 1863, Ward and another prisoner swam from the rocks of the Island to their freedom in Lane Cove. Despite the shark infested waters of Sydney Harbour and the known depths not being enough of a deterrent, some were still willing to risk life and limb to make the journey.

However, Frederick Ward wasn't the first to ignore the dangers. Some five years earlier, in 1858, John Peisley was also prepared to take the risk.

June 1858

ATTEMPTED ESCAPE OF THREE CONVICTS FROM COCKATOO ISLAND

On Tuesday morning [8th June] at about half past seven o'clock, three convicts attempted to escape from Cockatoo Island by swimming to the Lane Cove side of the Parramatta River. These prisoners shortly after having been turned out took up a hand cart and proceeded round the island in the vicinity of the sentry box beneath the flagstaff; observing no one near, they stripped themselves and concealed their clothes in the hand cart.

They were on the point of jumping in the water when they were noticed by a convict named Docking, who happened to be passing at the time. He immediately ran and informed the police and the superintendent of the island. Meanwhile the three men had plunged into the water and had swum nearly half way across before the boats were fairly in pursuit.

A number of the police proceeded to the point nearest in a direct line to the position of the men in the water and fired several rounds of ball cartridge at them, some of the bullets ricocheting within a few inches of the men in the water.

During the progress of the firing, the guard boat went in pursuit with three policemen in it, as also two other boats - one of them the provision boat, the other a spare boat, was manned with two or three policemen. The firing was continued until all chance of escape was cut off and if our information be correct, for some time after it was absolutely justifiable.

When the prisoners were fairly captured they were not permitted to get into the boats, but were commanded at the peril of their lives to remain in the water, holding on in a state of complete exhaustion to the stern of the provision boat; indeed one of the men had partially succeeded in getting into the bow of the provision boat, when he was forced into the water again.

The whole of the boats formed into a convoy, and escorted the prisoners to the shore, when some of the free officers of the island - not altogether destitute of humanity - helped the men out of the water. The whole of the men where so prostrated with the intense cold, and the exertion necessary to support themselves in the water, that they were quite exhausted on reaching the shore.

This attempt at escape is to be attributed to the absence of the sentry at the station under the flag-staff, which, when the island was guarded by the military, was regularly occupied by a sentry.

This very extraordinary occurrence in the broad light of day calls for investigation at the hands of the Government. If, as has been openly stated through the city, the firing was continued long after all chance of escape had been cut off, this is a still more cogent reason why the public should be informed as quickly as possible of the real state of the case, as not only the discipline and guardianship of the island are involved, but also the humanity of certain members of the police who compose that guard. A policeman has since been placed on sentry at the station under the flag-staff.

— Empire, 10 June 1858, page 4

The three convicts in question were Henry East - serving twelve years for armed robbery, Frederick Nowlan (aka Samuel Naters) – another of Bathurst's highway robbers, serving ten years for robbery and John Peisley.

The escape attempt was the subject of heated debate in the Parliament, with the Colonial Secretary (Charles Cowper) being asked to explain the actions of the guards. His response was written as follows:

June 1858

> PARLIAMENTARY SUMMARY - In reply to a question from Mr Flood, the Colonial Secretary said that it *was* true as reported in last week's Bell's Life, that three of the bandits at Cockatoo, tired of their insular seclusion, had attempted to escape by swimming.
>
> It was *not true* that the Cockatoo guards kept up their harmless fusillade after the recapture of the prisoners; it was *not true* that the ball practice of the said guards was to take aim with both eyes shut; it was *not true* that the prisoners, upon climbing into the boats, were knocked kicking into the briny element again.
>
> With respect to other items relative to other matters published in Bell, the (Col Sec) was of opinion that the guard *could* put a bullet into a haystack, afloat or ashore. It was *not* the intention of Government to strike a medal for distribution amongst the police for their gallantry; and so far from any brutality having been displayed towards the unhappy brigands, the Super-in-splendour

> and other principal officers in the island were so rejoiced to welcome them back, that they gave them a helping hand out of the water, and treated them in the most considerate manner, to dry clothing, drams of brandy, coffee, muffins, &c.
>
> — Bell's Life in Sydney and Sporting Reviewer, 19 June 1858, page 2

For his escape attempt, Peisley received the sentence from Ormsby - to spend the next nine months in irons. However fortunate, six months later the residue of his punishment was relaxed in January 1859, but worse was to come.

In March, after refusing to work he was sentenced to fourteen days in the "cells".

The sentence to irons later worked against him when he applied for a ticket of leave two years later in September 1860, it finally being issued at the end of November. In this ticket of leave he was restrained to the district of Scone.

Lambing Flat Riots

In the middle of 1861, the Western Districts of New South Wales were in turmoil. Several disturbances had taken place at Lambing Flat (now known as Young), a gold mining area just west of the Abercrombie Mountains.

The turmoil was largely bought about by the Legislative Council in Sydney rejecting the anti-Chinese bill, and a simultaneous rumour that a new group of fifteen hundred Chinese miners were on the road to the goldfields.

In Lambing Flat the miners united, with the European, North America and Australian-born miners banding together to attack the Chinese miners already present in the goldfields. The most notorious of these disturbances occurred on the night of 30 June 1861 when a riot took place involving thousands of miners who not only destroyed property, but they also fought physically and violently. Although nobody was killed, it was largely agreed that the first shot in the affray was indeed fired by the police.

The consequence of the unrest at Lambing Flat was for the Government to send a strong contingent of police to the area to restore order. They stayed for the next twelve months, effectively keeping the tinderbox at bay and avoiding what could have become the New South Wales version of the deadly Eureka Rebellion that had occurred at Ballarat in Victoria some six years earlier.

In the month following the riot, there was heavy criticism in the press of the government's inaction in policing the goldfields, with accusations made that the existing local constabulary was ill-equipped and insufficient to effectively protect and maintain order. The discussion made it's way to Parliament who proposed a new Police Act that centralised the management of the rural police forces, taking this role away from the district magistrates who were, until then, able to direct the hiring and firing of police. In short, the proposed Police Regulation Bill was such:

November 1861

THE POLICE REGULATION BILL

…it is proposed to discontinue making the increase of pay the result of promotion from one grade to another, and for which advancement every member of the force will have an opportunity of qualifying himself.

The spirit of honourable ambition will be thus largely awakened."

— The Maitland Mercury and Hunter River General Advertiser, 30 November 1861, page 2

In line with the Bill, the policing of New South Wales was to be divided into districts, which in the case of Western New South Wales was to be known as the "Western District" encompassing Bathurst, Orange, Molong, Wellington, Dubbo, Carcoar, Mudgee and Rylstone – the management of which would be centralised in Bathurst under the control of an individual named Frederick Pottinger who was later appointed as the district's Inspector. Pottinger's role in the policing of the district went on to infamy. Today, Pottinger's nickname is still part of the Australian vernacular - "Blind Freddy".

The proposed change in Police regulations which saw its members having to demonstrate their worthiness to get promotions and pay increases, seems to have met its desired action. The crime reports in the local newspapers amped up, with almost every incident being prominently attributed with the name of the constable or trooper leading the charge. Similarly, the police magistrates, such as Carcoar's Owen Beardmore, who were to be effectively sidelined and for all intents, to be made powerless, had to demonstrate their importance.

Up until that time, the local police force in the area east of Lambing Flat was largely made up by British born Sergeant John Middleton, then in his thirties, and Scottish born Trooper William Hosie, also in his thirties, who were stationed at Tuena.

Their duties involved everything from policing of mining licenses to the apprehension of criminals, the latter then transported to the Carcoar watchhouse. In Tuena, Middleton and Hosie were well regarded in the dispense of their duties:

March 1861

> TUENA - Too much praise cannot be given to Middleton and Hosie for the promptness and zeal with which they discharge their duties. Our Police Magistrate resides about 30 miles away, and visits us but once a month."
>
> — Bathurst Free Press and Mining Journal, 6 March 1861, page 2

In Carcoar, the residing Police Magistrate – at the time Owen Beardmore – decided the fate of those bought before him, and those he felt warranted, were then relayed to Bathurst for trial.

Apart from being recorded as a major incident in Australia's colonial history, the Lambing Flat riots were to have a resounding impact on the entire law system and the actions of those who worked in that system, on both sides of the law.

Middleton and Hosie would later play key roles in the demise of John Peisley.

On the run

In the months preceding the Lambing Flat riots and following his second release from Cockatoo Island in November 1860, John Peisley's flagrant disregard for rules continued. Not one week had elapsed till he again appeared in the crime lists. This time he was at Gunning Flat, near Burrowa, only forty or so kilometres away from Lambing Flat, but hundreds of kilometres south of his designated restraining district of Scone in New South Wales.

In early December 1860, Peisley was accused of being in the company of two other criminals when they robbed a man in his home in the Binalong district. This is the first of his crimes that appeared to involve firearms, so several years at Cockatoo Island taught him nothing of the difference between good and bad.

The following months saw the Peisley name attached to many crimes in the same area and beyond:

Robbing right and left

February 1861

BINALONG - The house of Johanna Hanrigan, of Gunning Flat, near Burrowa, was robbed on the night of the 15th instant, by three armed men, of about £7 in silver, amongst which was a three-penny piece, dented, and with a hole, (can be identified), and two small sized odd percussion pistols.

Description —1st, about 5 feet 9 inches high, rough voice, supposed to be a native, wore blue shirt, moleskin trousers, dark California hat, and had crape over his face.

2nd, about 5 feet 7 inches high,... yellow looking moleskin trousers and California hat.

3rd, about 5 feet 6 inches high, light hair, inclined to red, red bushy whiskers, fresh complexion, sharp spoken. They rode three good horses, and supposed to have gone towards the Abercrombie, Tuena, or Carcoar; the 3rd man is named John Peisley, a ticket-of-leave holder out of his district.

— New South Wales Police Gazette and Weekly Record of Crime, 25 February 1861, page 2

March 1861

> TUENA - The notorious Peisley has it appears, in concert with other villains been robbing right and left, and on Friday morning early, or rather, between Thursday night and Friday morning, our indefatigable serjeant Middleton, with trooper Hosie, brought in two men with whom they previously had some acquaintance, having some days since accidentally fallen in with them, and passed them by as honest men, but subsequently finding they were deceived, again tracked them, but only found their horses and swags, which they conveyed to Carcoar, and upon investigation the proceeds of a small robbery belonging to a travelling jeweller appeared among the contents.
>
> — Goulburn Herald,
> 6 March 1861, page 3

Sergeant Middleton and Trooper Hosie would later figure prominently in the life of John Peisley, but until then and despite their efforts to track him down, Peisley would continue to evade them.

March 1861

THE ABERCROMBIE ROBBERIES

The Carcoar Correspondent of the Bathurst Times states that two of the fellows who have recently been committing a series of robberies about the Abercrombie have been captured by Middleton and Hosie of Tuena, and are now under remand, in the lock-up at Carcoar. ... Peisley is reported still at large, but it is thought he will shortly be in durance vile.

— The Sydney Morning Herald,
9 March 1861, page 5

May 1861

DISTRICT OF BATHURST - FIFTY POUNDS REWARD

On Saturday, the 23rd ultimo, Mr Richard Cox Shaw, an officer of the Bank of New South Wales, was fired at and robbed of his horse, together with £565 in £5 and £1 notes, with gold and silver, when proceeding from Louisa Creek to Tambaroora, by two men, supposed to be John Peisley, a ticket-of-leave holder, described and reported in this issue as being illegally at large from his District and William Campbell, alias McKenzie, alias

Scotchy Hand, alias Big Mouthed Scotchy...

— New South Wales Police Gazette and Weekly Record of Crime, 2 May 1861, page 1

June 1861

ORANGE

In the absence of the Chief and ordinary constables, two worthies visited Mr Dalton's inn, Byng street [Orange], on Friday night, and partaking of some liquors, watched the opportunity to make an attempt to open, by skeleton keys, the drawer where mine host usually keeps some money; but Mrs Dalton having occasion to enter the room, was astonished to find a man thus engaged, and courageously collared the ruffian, and gave the alarm. Mr D and a man-servant ably seconded in the capture, and after some difficulty in finding a policeman, the prisoner was secured in the lock-up. The accomplice of the prisoner disappeared just before the detection of his "pal." A short time after the above occurrence, a suspicious looking individual called at Mr Dalton's to enquire after his "mates," but Mr D having just had a sample of their kind intentions to relieve him from the care of his cash, gave him a cool reception, and the fellow decamped. Mr Dalton shrewdly suspects the man to be the notorious "Peisley," for whose apprehension a reward of £100 [£50] is offered, and he justly complains that two troopers lodged at a neighbouring inn declined to aid in the apprehension, or search for the gang that had evidently visited Orange. In the early part of the evening, one of the rascals told Mrs Dalton that their last visit to this town was at the "election" — the very time that Mr W T Evans' iron safe was broken open and robbed of its contents.

— Bathurst Free Press and Mining Journal, 5 June 1861, page 2

The accusations weren't limited to press speculations. In June 1861, an inquest was held into the death of John Watt at Wallbrook who was shot multiple times at close range. As a witness to Watt's movements prior to being shot, a man called Michael Walsh provided evidence. Walsh had previously been in the employ of Watt.

June 1861

CADE OF MURDER

Michael Welsh (sic Walsh) said, that about 8 o'clock on Saturday night, he and Watt left Badley's house at Jeremy and started on horseback for Wallbrook, a distance of about fourteen miles; when they had travelled about ten miles they saw three men coming in the opposite direction; he said to Watt, "here is Peisley and his party coming against us, and the best thing we can do is to turn back". Watt said he (Walsh) might turn back but he should go on ahead. He (Walsh) a fortnight before that was on his way to Baldwin's when he met a man named Patrick Hogan, who told him that Peisley had sworn upon the book that the first time he met him (Walsh) he would shoot him.

— Bathurst Free Press and Mining Journal, 29 June 1861, page 2

The inquest determined Watt's death to be wilful murder, and Walsh, it appears, was trying to implicate John Peisley as the murderer. A week later, Walsh himself was remanded on suspicion of the murder. At his trial in September, the defence tried to steer the jury towards Peisley and other bushrangers as being the perpetrators. Walsh was defended by Arthur Holroyd, and it is noted that both Middleton and Hosie gave testimony in his defence. Walsh was subsequently found not guilty and released. The accusations continued with John Peisley's name being placed against many supposed crimes despite those crimes being hundreds of kilometres apart.

At times, merely being associated with John Peisley – in his company or not – was enough to brand you a demon.

July 1861

ROCKLEY

On Saturday last a man named John Cosgrove passed through Rockley enroute for Bathurst, being in the custody of two troopers. Cosgrove's name has been mentioned freely for some time in connexion with the notorious Peisley and there can be little doubt that they are mixed up in some way or other.

I am not aware whether any definite charge in this respect has as yet been preferred against Cosgrove, but I understand that he is now charged with cattle-stealing.

— Bathurst Free Press and Mining Journal, 24 July 1861, page 2

And then, in what could be construed as the 1860s version of click-baiting, seemingly benign press reporting was at times spiced up with mentions of John Peisley.

August 1861

GOLDFIELDS - MOUNTAIN RUN - We last evening received reliable information that between 600 and 800 diggers are at present located on the Mountain Run Creek. The diggings, extend to that part of the Abercrombie which is said to be the rendezvous of the bushranger Peisley, and we are informed that considerable alarm on the part of the few diggers who first went there to dig evinced itself, until the population was increased.

— Freeman's Journal, 10 August 1861, page 5

August 1861

The report that I have mentioned above about Bushrangers being out in the neighbourhood of Bogolong and Weego is true, as a messenger came into town yesterday with the information that four men were out in that direction. They had bailed up and robbed Mr McGuire's station at the Pinacle, taking all the money they could find, stripping the men, and dragging them in that condition two miles into the bush, another man they stopped on the road, stripping him also and leaving him in that state. It is said that Peisley is with this mob, also Gardiner who was supposed to have been shot by Middleton...

— Bathurst Free Press and Mining Journal, 31 August 1861, page 2

Note: This is likely John McGuire, co-owner of Sandy Creek Station with Ben Hall. McGuire was married to Ellen, the sister of Biddy Hall and Kitty Walsh.

July 1861

BUSHRANGING

It has been our duty lately, frequently to record the exploits of a gang of daring villains who have for some time past been levying "black mail" upon the residents of Caloola, Rockley, and other places in that quarter, and although the outcry has been loud, and protection from these outrages been frequently and urgently demanded, yet, we are not aware that any very active or energetic steps have been taken, either to apprehend the depredators or to present a recurrence of their visits. The man Peisley has the credit of having organised a gang of desperadoes in the neighbourhood of the Abercrombie, and of course, all the cases of bushranging which have recently occurred have been charged to his account.

— Bathurst Free Press and Mining Journal,
20 July 1861, page 2

Some accused men even found themselves guilty of crimes by mere association or having known Peisley at some point, or by their supposed crimes being in the vicinity of or conducted in the same the manner as John Peisley.

Then an event in mid July 1861 left nobody in doubt.

July 1861

TUENA – BUSHRANGERS

On Thursday last, the greatest excitement prevailed here in consequence of the arrival of an aboriginal lad from Bigga with intelligence that Sergeant Middleton, and Trooper Hosie were both wounded in their attempt to capture some villains at Fogg's on the Fish River, supposed to be a portion of the gang of marauders who have so long caused terror to the settlers and peaceable inhabitants residing in the Western Districts.

— Bathurst Free Press and Mining Journal, 24 July 1861, page 2

This event involved the bushranger Frank Gardiner, and it is likely that John Peisley wasn't anywhere near it, however, by the efforts of Trooper Hosie, Peisley's name was to be placed front and centre.

Fogg's Hut

The details of the incident that took place at the residence of William Fogg on the Fish River are clouded in a mixture of press reports and court transcripts. The press reported reasonably quickly, based on information supposedly received from Constable Middleton and Trooper Hosie, the policemen based at Tuena, which gave it some credence.

Follows is a summary of how it played out, at least in the press in the days following the event. Scattered among the reports are statements saying that Middleton was shot dead. Others say that Frank Gardiner was also shot dead. Neither of these were true.

On Monday 15 June 1861, the police officers from Tuena – Sergeant John Middleton and Trooper William Hosie – left Tuena and headed on horseback toward Fish River, some thirty kilometres west. They had received information from residents at Bigga that the home of a man named as William Fogg, about four miles from Bigga, was the rendezvous point for bushrangers, notably Peisley's gang.

Arriving at Fogg's hut around eleven on the following morning, Sergeant Middleton was the first to enter, finding only Mrs Mary Fogg. She denied that anyone else was in the house, however Middleton ascertained that a man was present in a room off the main room. Reports vary on whether the room had a locked door or the entry was draped with a curtain. The man in the room was Frank Gardiner.

Gardiner yelled to Middleton that he would shoot the first person to enter the room. Undeterred, Middleton entered and soon came under fire. He received four wounds, one in the mouth, two in the leg, and one through the hand. He then fired at Gardiner, the bullet either entering his left side or grazing his head. Reports from this point on, differ widely.

Hearing the gunshots, Trooper Hosie then came in, although other reports say that Gardiner ran out of the house and was confronted by Hosie. According to Hosie, Gardiner fired at him, the ball striking his head and another passing up his arm, his wounds later described as "slight". Hosie was knocked to the ground. From behind, the injured Middleton rushed at Gardiner and after a struggle, managed to take him down by beating Gardiner's head with the butt of a pistol. With this, Middleton managed to secure Frank Gardiner. According to Hosie's account, he then sent the injured and exhausted Middleton to Bigga to receive medical assistance and send help, while he held Gardiner prisoner at Fogg's.

Then the story gets murky. After Middleton left, William Fogg returned home to find his friend Gardiner in the custody of Hosie. Fogg apparently stated that Peisley and his gang were due back at the house and would surely rescue Gardiner. Determined not to wait for help, Hosie then put Gardiner on a horse, and along with William Fogg, decided to head to the McGuiness residence a short distance away. Some accounts say they overtook Middleton, who had lost his way and they had all proceeded together. Other accounts say that Middleton struggled with Gardiner, trying to strike him with the butt of his whip, but was stopped by Fogg. Then it is claimed that John Peisley arrived and despite Hosie trying to prevent him taking off with Gardiner, and given their injuries, he was obliged to hand Gardiner over. He said that as Gardiner was being led off by Peisley, he (Hosie) took another shot at Gardiner, hitting him in the back. Fogg he said, took off with other members of Peisley's gang.

Finally reaching the residence of Thomas McGuiness at Bigga, Hosie and Middleton got medical attention. While Middleton's wounds were serious and potentially fatal, Hosie's wounds were superficial. Despite the doctor recommending Hosie remain quiet to rest, the following day the "unstoppable" Hosie again went out in pursuit. William Fogg and his wife Mary were arrested as accomplices and taken into custody at Carcoar, later to be released on bail.

The next day, further information on the affray made the press. This time it was claimed that Middleton never entered the room at Fogg's hut, but Gardiner – armed with two six-barrelled revolvers – commenced firing, so Middleton and Hosie fired back at random. How they ascertained that Gardiner had two revolvers is unknown, however they were no match for the police standard issue of longarm carbines or in the case of Middleton, an old fashioned pistol. There is no doubt that Middleton sustained the injuries described and immediately headed back to Bigga, leaving Hosie to deal with Gardiner and Fogg. One report then said that, upon taking both Gardiner and Fogg into custody (handcuffed) and proceeding to Bigga, he was met by Peisley and two mates, who then forced Hosie to free both.

Meanwhile, based purely on the press reports and without hesitation, the New South Wales police posted a reward for the apprehension of Gardiner (£20) and Peisley (£50), and a further £50 offered for information that would lead to their conviction. It was reported at this stage that Fogg was in custody at Carcoar, one report suggested that Gardiner was dead – another saying he was making a recovery.

While this was going on, there was criticism that the local Police Magistrate, Owen Beardmore, had not been to the district since April – it was now late July.

What is evident is that the incident described was shocking enough to have been reported in just about every major newspaper in Australia. In effect it was the perfect story to hit the headlines, hot on the heels of the criticism being voiced over the events at Lambing Flat a few weeks earlier. It was used widely as an example of the government's neglect and the peril faced by police in the Abercrombie area. In many cases, it was reported in the press alongside the reports from Lambing Flat, as if related.

The Fogg's Hut affair had everything – the attachment of known "villains" – Frank Gardiner in particular, and John

Peisley. It played into the "heroic" examples needed by police to retain their ranks in the face of the new Police Regulation Bill, and their required displays of "ambition."

Was the event at Fogg's Hut the "spirit of honourable ambition" Middleton and Hosie needed to demonstrate they were worthy of positions in the police force? It gave the embattled Police Magistrates something to argue.

In Bathurst and Carcoar, the result was to catapult Middleton and Hosie to celebrity status. The public responded, not so much with due empathy for their injuries, but with a reward for their heroism:

August 1861

> At a public meeting holden at Carcoar it was unanimously resolved to collect subscriptions for the purpose of offering a reward to Sergeant Middleton and Trooper Hosie, for their gallant and unflinching conduct in their late encounter with the bushrangers in the Abercrombie Mountains. Subscriptions will be received by the Bench of Magistrates at Carcoar and Bathurst.
>
> — Bathurst Free Press and Mining Journal, 10 August 1861, page 3

The fund raised more than £118 – well over a years' pay for a policeman in the day – despite Middleton and Hosie having caught no-one, and yet no one having gone to trial. The list of contributors read like a who's who of the Bathurst judiciary:

Owen Beardmore (Police Magistrate at Carcoar), Solomon Meyer JP (Storekeeper at Carcoar and later Politician), Captain John Gennys JP (Thomas Icely's son-in-law), Edward JC North JP, N Connolly Jun JP, A Lynch JP and His Honor Judge Dowling with many other contributions coming from townsfolk. However by far the largest contribution was received from Thomas Icely who gave £5. Icely was largely responsible for the incarceration of Thomas Peisley, the father of John Peisley, some thirteen years earlier.

Of the list of notables above, at least five of them (Beardmore, Meyer, North, Connoly and Lynch) would later sit on the bench in judgement of John Peisley, unanimously committing him to trial for murder. Beardmore had faced criticism from the press, who called for his dismissal for having allowed Peisley to remain at large for so long. A month after John's hanging, Beardmore resigned all his positions, sold his farm and left the district, later turning up in Queensland where he purchase a pastoral property with capital of £5000, a legacy left by relatives back in England. In Beardmore's history is a notable occurrence, that of his dismissal from employment in Canada some ten years earlier (1851) for having wilfully falsified the report of an investigation into the murder of three sailors. Sent to Australia, Beardmore was eventually to become a magistrate at Carcoar. Did he have something to prove?

What is apparent and perhaps glaring from the timing of events – the affair at Fogg's Hut on 16 July and the opening of the fund two weeks later – it appears the public, and indeed the judiciary, had already made up their mind. The version of events, as conveyed by Hosie, were judged correct. The only person charged at this point was William Fogg, who didn't front the court until the start of September. The criminals – Gardiner and Peisley – remained at large. Middleton and Hosie had caught no-one, and yet the town celebrated.

Bathurst Free Press and Mining Journal,
14 December 1861, page 3

William Fogg's trial

A few weeks after the incident, William Fogg faced trial charged with obstructing the police in the execution of their duties. The magistrate was Owen Beardmore, who by this time had returned to the district. The following accounts of the trial are taken largely as reported by the Bathurst Free Press and Mining Journal.

In giving his evidence, Middleton stated his version of events; that he went to Fogg's with the intention of apprehending Frank Gardiner who was illegally at large; that Gardiner was present in a room with a calico sheet for a door; that Gardiner threatened to shoot; that he entered the room and was indeed shot; that he returned fire.

He then stated that Hosie then came in and Middleton instructed him to try and shoot Gardiner from the back and that Gardiner then came out of the room and engaged in a fire fight with Hosie. Gardiner succeeded in wounding Hosie and then rushed at Middleton, the struggle resulting in Middleton hitting Gardiner over the head with the butt of his whip. When the struggle moved outside, Middleton then said that William Fogg tried repeatedly to get between him and Gardiner. Eventually, Gardiner was overtaken by Hosie who handcuffed him.

Continuing, Middleton then testified that Fogg and his wife helped the officers get Gardiner back into the hut. Middleton then searched the hut looking for any others, then asked Fogg to get someone to go to Bigga for help – to which he said there was no one who could find the way. He then asked Fogg for the loan of a horse, which Fogg refused. Middleton then left for Bigga by himself leaving Hosie in charge of

Gardiner. He said he was so confused due to his injuries that he lost his way, the trip which should have taken an hour and a half, took four or five hours. He then stated that he did not ask Fogg for help in taking Gardiner, and that until that day, he had never seen Gardiner, relying on a description he had, and the fact the Mary Fogg called him Frank Gardiner. He admitted that he did not have a warrant for Gardiner's arrest, nor did he identify his authority, saying that he was simply "dressed as a police officer".

He testified that it was Fogg who convinced Gardiner to allow himself to be handcuffed, and that when he left for Bigga he thought Gardiner was dying. He did not hear Gardiner call on Fogg for help. He recalled Fogg saying "Thank God the others are not here."

Then it was William Hosie's turn to give his version of events, which differed from Middleton's. He clarified that Middleton's initial instruction was to try and enter the house from the back, which he could not, so he entered from the front. After exchanging some gunshots in which he received wounds, he then rushed at Gardiner who was about to hit Middleton with the butt of a gun. By this time the struggle had moved outside. Hosie managed to disarm Gardiner and noted that Fogg had tried to prevent Middleton from striking Gardiner with a whip.

Hosie stated their reason for being at Fogg's was to search for bushrangers and that Gardiner was wanted for mail robbery. He did not know that Gardiner was illegally at large or had broken bail.

Hosie stated that William Fogg and his wife helped to get Gardiner back into the house and that Fogg himself offered to put the handcuffs on Gardiner. He went on to say that Fogg then showed him through to house to see if anyone else was there. Finding no-one Hosie left for Bigga for help, with both Gardiner and Fogg in tow. At one point in that journey Hosie, due to his injuries, was feeling faint and asked Fogg to take charge of Gardiner, which he did. When Hosie recovered he found Gardiner in the same place as he left him.

Gardiner and Hosie then got involved in a struggle, Gardiner getting away and racing toward a river, but returning with a tree branch that he intended to fight Hosie with. After again firing at Gardiner, Hosie overcame him and said that Fogg helped him return to the house, with Gardiner. He then again asked Fogg to help get Gardiner to Bigga which he agreed, finding a horse for himself and one for Gardiner.

Hosie's claim

While the events to this point as relayed by both Middleton and Hosie differ somewhat, the differences are not material. However, what happened after this relies on the testimony of Hosie, and it was this that was to have a profound effect on the life of John Peisley.

Hosie stated that while riding with Gardiner and Fogg back to Bigga, some three miles out from Fogg's, they were attacked by Peisley and one other, who demanded that Fogg let go of Gardiner's horse. Hosie said he believed the man to be Peisley. Firing his last shot at Peisley (assumed missing), Hosie then said Peisley and his mate held him at gunpoint, with Fogg pleading with them not to shoot and to spare Hosie his life. He testified that it was only with Fogg's help that they left – with Gardiner – leaving Hosie unharmed.

Cross examined, Hosie explained that he had been to Fogg's hut once before. He stated that Fogg had assisted with the apprehension of Gardiner and that Fogg did nothing towards rescuing Gardiner from beginning to end. He also admitted that he did not identify himself as a policeman (some news reports suggest that both Middleton and Hosie were wearing long knee length ponchos over their uniforms).

For all intents, Hosie had just defended William Fogg. Before allowing the case to be summed up, the magistrate (Beardmore) then called a halt to the case saying there was insufficient evidence to proceed any further. Fogg was released.

The Bathurst Times however, reported slightly differently, and perhaps a more colourful account, for which they cited Middleton and Hosie as the direct sources. The report is transcribed here for the sake of details, and because Middleton later said, at Frank Gardiner's trial, that he could not recall exactly what happened:

September 1861

> On the 16th July, having received information that Gardiner was to be at any time at Fogg's farm (distant from Bigga about three miles), I proceeded with trooper Hosie about 9 o'clock in the morning with the hope of falling across him, or any of the miscreants who might be there. Although I had received the information, I was not at all sanguine of falling in with him, as we had been on the hunt for several weeks previously.

However, when we came within a short distance of Fogg's hut, I thought it advisable to be careful in our approach so that no-one might escape. The country round the hut is scattered with stunted bush and I carefully kept out of the bushes between myself and the hut, trooper Hosie using the same preservation. When within about a dozen yards of the hut door, a woman suddenly made her appearance and as soon as she saw us approaching she threw up her arms in alarm, as if warning someone in the hut of our approach. I said to Hosie "Look out, there is somebody in the house" and immediately rode right up and dismounted, leaving Hosie to put up the sliprail.

I threw the bridle of my horse over the side of a dray that was standing close to the house and walked in. As I went in, I saw a calico screen, which parted another room from the outer one, fall down, and a voice from inside said "I'll blow out the brains of the first man that comes in here."

When I lifted the screen I saw Gardiner standing with a revolver presented at the entrance; he immediately fired but his shot did not take effect. I dropped the screen for an instant, as I was convinced that he "meant business." I however, again raised the calico and fired at him. Gardiner fired at the same moment, and the reports were so simultaneous that I thought my pistol had misfired. I felt a sudden pang and found that I had been shot in the mouth. I again dropped the screen and thinking that my pistol had not gone off, put on another cap, during which time Gardiner pointed his pistol at me through the slabs, but appearing not to be certain of his aim, he did not fire. When my pistol was capped, I went again to the screen, pulled the trigger and again the infernal pistol missed fire – as it might well do seeing that it has been discharged. Gardiner blazed away at me without any hesitation, wounding me in the left hand, left leg and in the inside of the left knee.

Finding that my pistol was of no use, and not feeling inclined to be riddled without a chance of returning Mr Gardiner's warm compliments, I retreated to the door of the hut, where I stationed myself with a heavily load whip, determined to do the best I could with that weapon. All that I have related only occupied an incredible short space of time.

Hosie who had been putting up the sliprail, now hurried up and said "Is this the game?" I told him not to go inside, but to go to the rear of the house and try to effect and entrance there. Hosie saw that I was wounded and covered with blood. He at once rushed behind the house but not being able to effect an entrance, came back almost immediately, and I said "Have a go in here."

Without any hesitation he went in the door and seeing Gardiner, fired at him, cutting him across the mouth. Gardiner fired at the same moment and the ball took effect in Hosie's head, who tumbled like a bullock that had been felled with a pole-axe. I imagined that the poor fellow had received his quietus and expecting that my own time was come also, determined to have another try with my whip. I made a strike at Gardiner's head but whether it was from weakness or from some other cause, the blow which I thought would have killed an ox, took but little effect upon him and we stood glaring at each other like a couple of wild beasts.

To my utter astonishment and joy all at one, I found that Gardiner was seized from behind by Hosie, who had been but momentarily stunned by the bullet which I thought had sent him to his last account. Gardiner struggled like a tiger, and knowing as I did, the desperate character we had to deal with, I deliberately took aim with my heavy whip, intending to knock his brains out, and but for the interference of Fogg, who interposed his arm, I have no doubt that I should have effectively put an end to his career in this world. Hampered by the burly frame of Fogg, I with difficulty got a blow at the desperate bushranger.

Hosie however managed to get the revolver with which Gardiner had done such execution, and threw him to the ground. Gardiner appeared by this time to be either dying or dead, but it proved afterwards that he had been shamming. I threw Hosie my handcuffs, which he immediately put upon our prisoner.

From the commencement of the fray to this time only occupied a dew minutes, but I began to be very faint from loss of blood and felt the necessity of getting some assistance. I demanded a horse from Fogg to remove the prisoner to Bigga, but he refused to lend one, and as I felt sure that Gardiner's mates would not be long away, I determined to proceed at once to Bigga, for assistance, leaving Hosie to

> guard the prisoner in the meantime. Weak, faint and suffering from the pain of my four wounds, I started for assistance, but being confused I lost myself in the bush and did not find my way to Bigga for nearly four hours, when I totally prostrated. I know nothing of what occurred to Hosie after I left him with the prisoner.

The article then continued with further descriptions added by Trooper Hosie:

> Hosie says - After Middleton left, I found that no assistance arrived for more than three hours, and after using threats and persuasions, I at last prevailed upon Fogg to get a horse for Gardiner (who was not at all desperately wounded). We all started for Bigga together, Fogg and Gardiner in advance, myself following. When about two miles from Fogg's, Peisley and another mounted man suddenly came up out of the bush and ordered that Gardiner should be instantly released, the men covering my body with pistols. Wounded, giddy and badly armed, I said nothing and the fellows took Gardiner's bridle and rode off with him, followed by Fogg.

> Determined not to let them go without another shot, I fired and I believe I hit

Gardiner in the back, as he fell forward on the saddle. Peisley fired at me, and the bullet whizzed by my head and he was going to fire again when Fogg said to Peisley "Don't kill him, or you will get me in for it" upon which they all rode away together, and I went on to Bigga, where I found Middleton, and where our wounds were at once attended to.

— Empire, 3 September 1861, page 5

From the above, apart from the flowery language used, of note is the timeframe spoken by Hosie, particularly the three hours elapsed in the front room of Fogg's hut, while he sat with both Gardiner and Fogg. This contrasts with his court testimony where he stated that they left for Bigga soon after he checked that Fogg's hut was clear.

The court testimony raises some unanswered questions. If Middleton went to Fogg's hut with the express intention of apprehending Gardiner, why did he not have a warrant? He stated that Gardiner was "illegally at large" – however this was not the case, Gardiner was constrained to the Carcoar district which included Bigga. In the later trials of Frank Gardiner (May and July 1864) magistrate Owen Beardmore testified that he told Middleton that Gardiner was wanted for robbery and Middleton testified that he had been specifically instructed to bring him in by Beardmore. Both testified that Middleton did not have a warrant, with Beardmore stating that he didn't give a warrant because Middleton didn't ask for one.

Why did Hosie not know that was why they went to Foggs? Having never seen Gardiner, why did Middleton rely purely on Mrs Fogg's identification? If he did not enter the side room, who exactly did Middleton think he was shooting at?

At Frank Gardiner's trial, some questions were raised as to the dress of both Middleton and Hosie, which confirmed they were both wearing cabbage tree hats, blue shirts and trousers, which Middleton described as their "undress" uniform, going on to say that he could not recall if he was wearing a poncho, despite describing the weather as cold and wet. He said he "thought he looked like a policeman", however he also said that he did not specifically identify himself as such to Gardiner or anyone in the house. Hosie testified that he and possibly Middleton were wearing ponchos that covered their clothing to the knee. So is it reasonable to question who Gardiner thought he was dealing with?

What is unclear is at what point William Fogg arrived – he was reportedly not in the house when Middleton first entered. At Frank Gardiner's trial it was revealed there was also another man at the farm who was working for William Fogg.

There are also reasonable concerns as to the impartiality of the magistrate, Beardmore, who at the time of the Fogg's trial was actively leading the drive to collect funds to reward Middleton and Hosie for their heroism and bravery.

Regardless, it was Hosie's testimony that John Peisley had released Gardiner that became his nemesis.

Cohorts

Frank Gardiner

Many books have been written which detail the history of Frank "Darkie" Gardiner, one of Australia's most notorious bushrangers. For that reason, the following is just a precis.

Born Francis Christie in the 1830s in Scotland (although his prison records state he was born in New South Wales), at the time of his criminal exploits he was described as handsome and charismatic, standing 5' 8" tall with an athletic build. He worked as a stockman in rural Victoria for a time, before being arrested for horse stealing and then sent to serve his time at Pentridge gaol in Melbourne. It didn't last. In 1851, Gardiner escaped from the gaol and eventually wound up at Yass in New South Wales, where he was caught selling stolen horses. He was then sentenced to time at Cockatoo Island in 1854. Here he met John Peisley.

After his release from Cockatoo in 1859, he was constrained to the Carcoar district, and by 1860 was running a butcher shop at Lambing Flat. He was likely at Lambing Flat during the riots of 1860 and 1861. Given the New South Wales police sent dozens of officers to Lambing Flat at that time, it is likely that he chose to clear out.

Following the events at Fogg's Hut in June 1861, Gardiner was charged with the attempted murder of Middleton and Hosie. How he evaded capture at that time is a matter of speculation. But it was his involvement in a robbery nearly a year later that claims his main fame.

Gardiner is most remembered for his involvement in the Eugowra robbery of the gold escort in 1862 – reputedly the largest gold heist in Australian history. This happened just six weeks after Peisley was hung at Bathurst. Teaming up with the notorious Ben Hall, it was this event that cemented Gardiner into the Australian history conversation.

Again, even the enormity of the Eugowra gold robbery didn't mean the police could catch him, despite them catching many of the bushrangers involved. Gardiner successfully evaded capture, remaining on the run until April 1864 when he was eventually apprehended in Queensland. A few months later he faced court on the attempted murder of Middleton charge, for which he was found not guilty, but then found guilty on the other charges. For this he received the enormous sentence of thirty two years in gaol. It was later commuted to ten years with his eventual release in 1874 being subject to him leaving Australia, which he did. As with many of the mysteries that have intrigued historians for decades, it is believe that he died in

America in around 1903 but records of his death don't appear to have been located.

Prior to John Peisley's death, Frank Gardiner was described as a member of the "Peisley gang". With Peisley now gone, the mantra became the "Gardiner gang" and every villain was in it. For all intents, as far as the press were concerned, the monster had just grown a new head, and Frank Gardiner's head was now firmly in their crosshairs.

William Fogg

Frank Gardiner's association with William Fogg is more than just as mates.

As a nineteen year old boy from Colchester in England, William Fogg was transported to Australia as a convict in 1832, to serve seven years for stealing some hats. He was consigned to work as a factory boy at Goulburn, however he soon absconded. Gaining his Certificate of Freedom in 1840, at Yass in 1842 he married Mary Annetta Taylor, the daughter of Adam and Sophia Taylor. Fogg was granted (let) occupation of over eleven hundred acres of land at Dirthole Flats in the Georgiana district of Western New South Wales. One of his neighbours was Tom McGuiness who had secured land at around the same time.

On his property, Fogg ran cattle but he was also said to have been a partner in the butchers shop at Lambing Flat with Frank Gardiner in 1860/61, perhaps a natural extension of running a cattle farm.

Following the events at his home (Fogg's Hut) where Middleton and Hosie were shot, William Fogg then became known as part of "Gardiner's gang". In May 1862, just a few days after John Peisley was hung, the press joyfully announced that William Fogg and his son William junior had been arrested, along with Fogg's brothers-in-law, Richard and William Taylor. The police it seemed, were on a roll. They charged the four men with murder, highway robbery and cattle stealing – or so it was reported. In fact, in November that year only William Fogg junior and William Taylor faced the court charged with assault and armed robbery. However, the case was weak, the claim unsubstantiated and the jury found them not guilty.

Less than six months later, William Fogg was again arrested for stealing a cow. In this case he was found guilty and served twelve months in Goulburn Gaol.

A Family Affair

Fogg and Gardiner were well known to each other, in fact many of Australia's notable bushranger families were related. For instance, Fogg's wife Mary was the sister of James Taylor – the man who would later become the husband of Bridget "Biddy" Hall, Ben Hall's ex-wife. Frank Gardiner would later run off with Biddy's sister, Catherine "Kitty" Walsh. The family relationships continued well beyond John Peisley's death and the events at Fogg's hut. Fogg's daughter Sophia married Thomas McGuiness junior – their granddaughter married John Peisley's nephew, John Drady.

Thomas McGuiness's brother-in-law was William Benyon, the man for whose murder John Peisley would hang.

Further cohorts of Gardiner included John Vane. John Peisley's niece, Mary Ann Ridley would later marry Vane's brother.

To look at Australia's most notorious bushrangers in isolation is a misnomer. Many were well known to each other, if indeed not related either before, during and after their exploits.

HOW THE BUSHRANGERS WERE RELATED

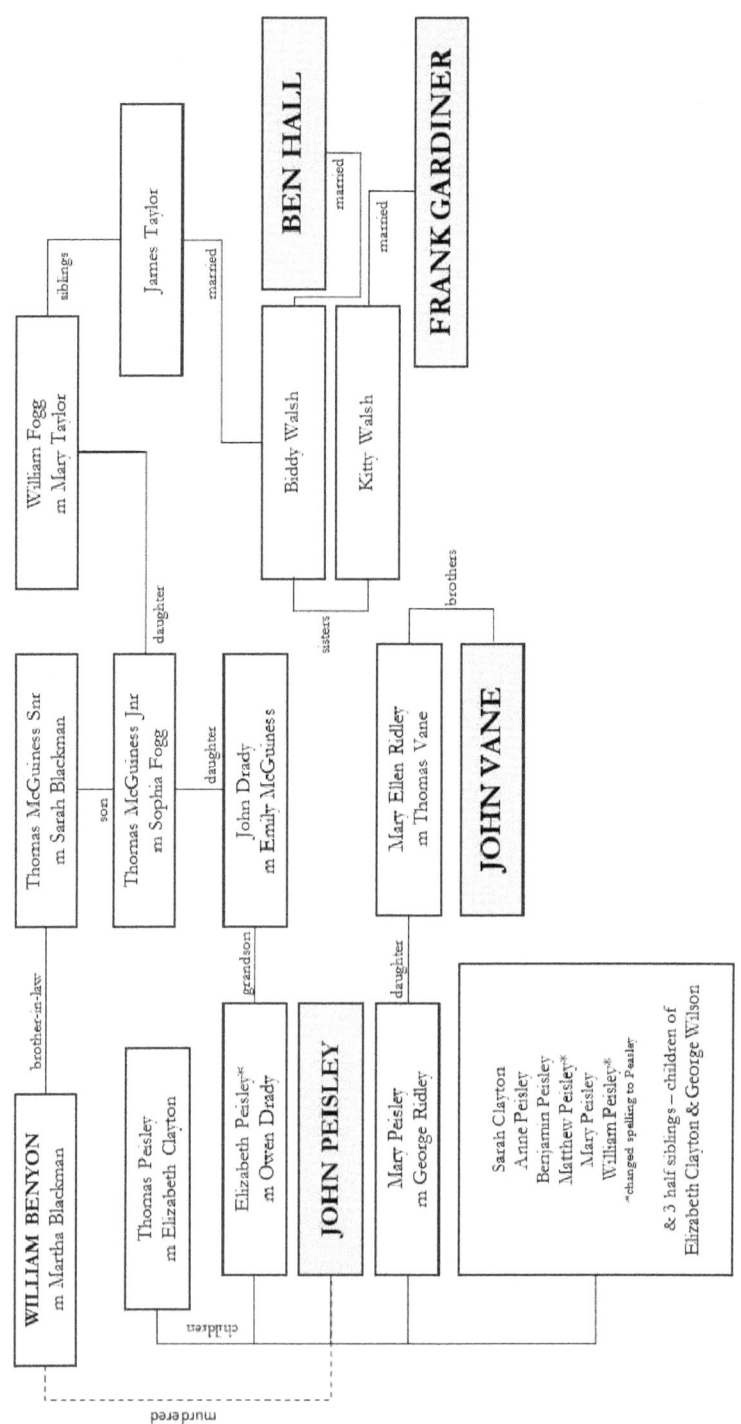

The Invisible Prince

Following the incident at Fogg's Hut, the police upped their ante. Under the charge "Attacking and wounding the Patrol with firearms" the reward for the capture of John Peisley now stood at £50 and the reward for information leading to his conviction was increased to £100. Frank Gardiner, who was also still at large, carried a reward of £20 for his apprehension only. It appears the New South Wales police were convinced of Hosie's story on the appearance of John Peisley and subsequent release of Gardiner while being taking into custody. At this point, the only witness to Peisley being anywhere near Fogg's hut was trooper Hosie.

Even with the enormity of the reward being offered, no-one in the area handed in either Gardiner or Peisley. This didn't deter the anyone though, with accusations against John Peisley continuing unabated, particularly in the NSW Police Gazette.

September 1861

> EDEN - 120 Chinese were stopped and robbed of the following property, about 2 miles from Bigga, on the road to Fish River, at 8am, on the 2nd ultimo, by four armed men, one of whom is known to be John Peisley.
>
> — New South Wales Police Gazette and Weekly Record of Crime, 16 September 1861, page 1

September 1861

> Vide Report of Crime of 25th July 1861 - A man answering the description of Gardiner, the bushranger, was seen at Jemalong on the 20th or 21st ultimo; he crossed the river, and went in the direction of the Bogan. He is supposed to carry several disguises with him, and represents himself as a squatter purchasing cattle. A man answering the description of Peisley, a mate of Gardiner, was seen at Jemalong about a week previous to the above date.
>
> — New South Wales Police Gazette and Weekly Record of Crime, 9 September 1861, page 2

September 1861

> On the morning of the 14th instant, Mr O'Sullivan of the Lachlan, was bailed up by armed men on his way from Marengo to Cowra, and taken into the bush and robbed, supposed to have been the notorious Peisley. Also, the hut of William Badkin situated at the Gap, near Marengo, was stuck up and one of the inmates named John Dawkins was robbed of £4 in notes. Description of the robbers—1st, about 6 feet high, dark complexion, black whiskers, supposed to be a native of the Colony; 2nd, an Irishman, low set, stout built, dark hair and whiskers, has a cast in one eye; both mounted. Supposed to be the same men who stuck up Mr O'Sullivan.
>
> — New South Wales Police Gazette and Weekly Record of Crime, 19 September 1861, page 2

At one point, the district of Yass was laying claim to Peisley and Gardiner robberies, claiming the bushrangers had left the Abercrombie and ventured south:

September 1861

> From information that has reached us we think it very likely that Peisley and his party have quitted the Abercrombie district and have honoured the southern

with their presence. One of the persons who knocked down and robbed Mr Blackshaw, at the Gap, last week, has been named as a confederate of Clarke's [Gardiner] and Peisley's, and therefore it is not improbable that both these men have crossed into our country, under the impression that they are safer here than in their old haunts. – Yass Courier

— Sydney Mail, 14 September 1861, page 3

Peisley was now being blamed for more than just provoking terror, the press assigned his name to everything from robbery to an economic downturn:

September 1861

Robberies during these last few months past have been so frequent that it would fill columns to give you an account of them.

At no period during these last twenty-five years have over such daring crimes been committed as at present, for the wretches, after robbing, ill-use their victims most unmercifully, and one noted character, named Peisley (for whom there is a large reward), has had the audacity to send a communication to one of the Bathurst papers denying his presence at a rescue that took place. From the repeated robberies lately it has become quite dangerous for any person to travel, and none will do so but those that are compelled. The consequence is that it has caused a great depression in trade.

The constables and mounted troopers are about in all directions, but they never succeed in apprehending any of these highwaymen, and I believe the magistrates have written to the Government for additional policemen for it appears now quite evident that they will not be caught with the present force at the disposal of the magistrates.

— The Sydney Morning Herald,
23 September 1861, page 7

The various accounts of John Peisley's activities in the Abercrombie, as widely reported, didn't go unnoticed by John Peisley himself. Still on the run for breaking his parole, Peisley himself took the extraordinary step of sending his own letter. The "communication" referred to in the previous quote was revealed in the Bathurst Free Press:

September 1861

To the Editor of the Bathurst Free Press and Mining Journal. Sir, — You will no doubt be surprised to receive a note (from the now by all accounts) noted Peisley, but Sir, through your valuable paper I must make it known that, if it be my lot to be taken, whether dead or alive, that I will never be tried for the rescue of Gardner, in the light in which it is represented, nor did I ever fire at Trooper Hosie. And such I wish to be known that it is in my power to prove what I here assert, and that beyond a doubt.

I am no doubt a desperado in the eyes of the law, but never, in no instance, did I ever use violence, nor did I ever use rudeness to any of the fair sex, and I must certainly be the Invisible Prince to commit one-tenth of what is laid to my charge.

And Sir, I beg to state that it is through persons in high positions that I now make this assertion, and trust I may never have to allude to it (again.) I love my native hills, I love freedom and detest cruelty to man or beast. Trusting you will publish this, my bold letter no doubt, but you can be assured it comes from the real John Peisley, and not any of my many representatives. I am, Mr Editor. Your much harassed Writer, JOHN PEISLEY. Fish River, Sept 4th 1861.

— Bathurst Free Press and Mining Journal,
14 September 1861, page 2

This letter prompted a swift reply from trooper Hosie, who a few days later wrote his own letter to the newspapers:

September 1861

> To the Editor of the Bathurst Free Press and Mining Journal. Sir, — Perceiving in your issue of this day, Saturday, September 14, a letter signed "John Peisley," and dated Fish River, 4th September, in which the writer states that "he will never be tried for the rescue of Gardiner in the light in which it is represented, nor did I ever fire at Trooper Hosie."
>
> I can only refer the public to the magisterial proceedings at Carcoar, in Fogg's case. Fogg never did, nor will he now, deny that Peisley was not the man who rescued Gardiner. It is certainly savouring of presumption on my part to doubt the authenticity of the signature, John Peisley, to the letter in question, but I should be glad, if within the compass of editorial latitude, unless all the circumstances of the late attempt at Peisley's and confederates capture, if you Mr Editor would kindly state whether the letter now published

came to your hands by post or otherwise, if the former through what post offices it passed on its way to Bathurst.

My duty to the public service and the general security of the public is always paramount to any published letter from a proscribed individual, his amanuensis, or a fictitious correspondent, assuming a genuine name, and that one not very creditable. Trusting you will find an odd corner for this letter, I am, Sir, Yours obediently, WILLIAM HOSIE. Tuena, Saturday Evening, September 14th, 1861.

(In reply to Mr. Hosie we may say, that the letter he refers to bears the stamp of genuineness, and we published it believing the signature to be that of the veritable John Peisley, and under the circumstances we have no hesitation in stating that the envelope bears the mark of the Carcoar Post-office. Ed. BFP)

— Bathurst Free Press and Mining Journal, 18 September 1861, page 2

Hosie's reply is telling in that while he vehemently defended his actions, he is more concerned with determining the veracity of the letter. There must, on his part, have been some sense of embarrassment that Peisley and Gardiner were still at large, however that is not his main concern. He must have questioned why, if Peisley was indeed in Carcoar – why no-one was helping to capture him, especially as the reward was so high and the news reports appearing almost daily.

In the following month, the reports of John Peisley's robbing ways kept up, with the newspapers continuing the pressure and accusations:

November 1861

> DARING ROBBERIES – Intelligence has reached town of three most daring robberies, perpetrated at Cook's Vale Creek, on the Tuena road on Wednesday night last, by three men, one of whom is supposed to be Peisley the bushranger.
>
> — Goulburn Herald,
> 6 November 1861, page 2

If all of the accounts are true, Gardiner and Peisley must have surely be riding the high life as their potential reapings were now heading into possibly thousands of pounds.

There are no visible reports of robberies in December 1861 that specifically mention Gardiner and Peisley, but that was to change come Christmas.

Benyon

On the 3rd of January 1862, William Benyon, a farmer located a few miles from Bigga, died from a gunshot wound inflicted by John Peisley. How his death came about is reported in various news articles and in detailed trial transcripts. When finally captured, John Peisley went to trial in March 1862. This story goes as follows.

On Boxing day 1861, John Peisley was in the Abercrombie where he visited his relative, Tom McGuiness. McGuiness ran a tavern on the banks of the Lachlan River, just south of Fogg's Hut, with his wife Sarah, son Thomas junior and other children.

On the way to McGuiness's Inn, Peisley caught up with a local man named James Wilson who ran a store on the Abercrombie, just along the road from the McGuiness Inn. In his later testimony, Wilson stated that he had known Peisley "for many years" with the likelihood they met at Bathurst Gaol in March 1854 when they were separately being tried for theft. Wilson also entered Cockatoo Island on the same day as Frank

Gardiner in April 1854 to later be joined by John. Wilson was issued a ticket of leave in 1856.

On the morning of 28th December, John Peisley and James Wilson left McGuiness's Inn at 7 am, headed for Fogg's Hut.

Later that afternoon, Peisley returned to the home of Tom McGuiness junior, his face covered with blood and his shirt torn. He asked for a clean shirt and told McGuiness that he had been fighting with the Beynon's, explaining that the gash on his head was the result of being hit with a shovel, a wound inflicted by Stephen Benyon. McGuiness said that in this meeting, Peisley appeared "like a half mad man", declared that he "had never done a cowardly act in his life" but then said he was about to go and shoot Stephen Benyon – not intending to kill him, but only to "wing" him. Peisley then left McGuiness, returning later and stating that he had shot William Benyon.

William Benyon was (in law) the uncle of Tom McGuiness who knew the Benyon's well. McGuiness then went to Benyon's farm – taking John Peisley with him. While Peisley waited outside Benyon's house with Wilson, McGuiness went in to check on William Benyon. He said there were eight or ten people present when Peisley was in the yard. Nobody attempted to arrest him.

One of the people present when Peisley shot William Benyon was his wife Martha. She knew Wilson, had heard of Peisley but until that time had not met him. When Peisley and Wilson first arrived at their farm earlier that day, Martha fetched William Benyon from the barn. The group then drank beer and wine together, while Martha's housemaid prepared a meal. During lunch, Peisley challenged William Benyon to run, jump, or fight, apparently to settle a "down" that Peisley had against

Benyon. This related to a horse swap that had occurred between the two some seventeen years earlier, at which time Peisley would have been nine or ten years old and Benyon nineteen. Benyon and Peisley then proceeded to physically fight.

Martha Benyon later testified that she heard her husband say "You struck me cowardly, don't do it again." to which Peisley replied "Come outside and have it out." They then went outside, and after fighting two or three rounds, fell to the ground together. William Benyon's brother, Stephen, then stepped between the two, fighting with Peisley who then ran back into the house. William Benyon also went back into the house followed by Martha. She declared she saw Peisley with his left hand round William's shoulders, and a knife in his right, as if about to stab him, the sight of which made her scream "my God, are you going to stab my husband?" Peisley then left the house, asked for a shirt – refusing one that was offered because it was not new – he then said he was off to Bigga to get one.

Before going outside to fight with William Benyon, Peisley had given his pistols to Wilson who laid them down on a hall table. Martha (or her housemaid) took them and hid them in the garden, later returning them when Peisley asked for them, before he left for Bigga.

He said to Benyon "Now I'm all right" which Benyon acknowledged and said "You don't mean to shoot us, do you ?", with Peisley replying "No, I never did a cowardly act in my life, and I don't mean to do one now." Peisley then left, presumably to go to Tom McGuiness's house for the new shirt.

About an hour and a-half later, Peisley was back and went to the barn where William Benyon was now working with his brother Stephen. They commenced fighting again and Peisley drew his revolver, taking a shot at William Benyon which hit him in the neck. Benyon was then taken into the house while, according to Martha, Peisley followed with a revolver in each hand. Tending to her husband, Martha sent a farm hand to McGuiness's Inn for wine and to ask for a doctor to be sent.

As with many stories of the day, the details differ somewhat according to who was recounting the events, and this was certainly the case with what happened in the barn. Martha was not there – she was in the house the whole duration of the fighting. In later testimony, a farm hand, who was there, stated that he also saw Peisley fighting with Stephen Benyon.

After Peisley left for Bigga the first time, the farmhand was working in the barn with Stephen. William Benyon came to the barn and handed Stephen a gun, before riding off on a horse. When Peisley returned, Stephen Benyon took the gun and aimed at Peisley. Smiling, Peisley said "What are you going to do with the gun!" Stephen said, "I understand you are coming to shoot us all?" to which Peisley replied "Oh no, did l ever do a cowardly act ?" Stephen said, " I never heard of you doing one." "Well then," said Peisley, "shake hands.'" They shook hands, and Stephen laid the gun down.

While giving his horse some hay, Peisley grabbed the gun and said to Stephen Benyon "Now, you bastard, it is my turn." and he immediately fired, hitting Stephen in the arm, or "winging" him. Stephen ran off and Peisley pointed the gun at him again, and pulled the trigger, but the gun misfired. He followed Stephen, but then William Benyon rode up. Peisley ordered him to dismount, saying, "Benyon, I mean to shoot you." Peisley marched Benyon into a yard, had the pistols pointed, and kept threatening to shoot him. William Benyon sprang toward Peisley and was within three feet of him when the Peisley shot him in the neck, and he fell.

Meanwhile, James Wilson recalled that after a night of drinking, on the day in question he was very drunk and could not remember anything that happened.

Stephen Benyon's version of events did not largely alter the previous summary. He admitted they fought. He admitted that he struck Peisley with a shovel. He also admitted that when Peisley returned to the barn, he threatened Peisley with a gun. He said that Peisley questioned what he was going to do with the gun, that he said he thought Peisley was back to shoot them all, to which Peisley replied "Nonsense, we are as good friends as ever." This prompted Stephen to put down the gun, but Peisley later snatched it up and shot him through the arm. Stephen said he then ran away and remained hidden in the bush the remainder of the afternoon.

According to later testimony, the only person in the yard who witnessed Peisley shooting William Benyon, was Martha Benyon's housemaid. She was threatened at gunpoint by Peisley before he shot William Benyon. He later mocked her for screaming "Oh, my poor master." She and others helped Benyon back into the house – with Peisley in tow, and they remained there for an hour. She said that Peisley had a pistol in each hand the whole time.

When William Benyon died six days later, there was no autopsy performed, the doctor assuming the gunshot wound to the neck was the cause of death. No inquest was held as the office of Coroner for the Carcoar district had been abolished only weeks earlier.

So, the only person to witness the actual shooting was Martha Benyon's housemaid which later raised some interesting questions. Testimony from James Wilson's wife, Jane Wilson, said that shortly before the trial, she heard Martha Benyon state that she "intended" for Peisley to hang – a point Martha later denied. The housemaid was questioned as to whether Martha had coached her by instructing that her testimony should also lead to Peisley's hanging. Both the maid and Martha denied having this conversation. A further detailed account of the trial is discussed in a later chapter.

Who was William Benyon?

William Benyon was a publican in Lower George Street, Sydney running the Butcher's Arms (previously the Vine Tavern) prior to his arrival in the Abercrombie region in the late 1850s. In Sydney he also ran a butcher shop, which appears to have been the domain of his wife Martha (nee Blackman). The couple had married in Carcoar in 1847, and the following year Martha inherited three blocks of land from her deceased father's estate, one of which was nearly two hundred acres of land at Bigga. Her father had a substantial sheep and cattle estate.

While in Sydney, Benyon was no stranger to trouble with the law, albeit for minor offences such as using foul language and on some occasions, threatening behaviour. In 1852 William and his brother Stephen were charged with a serious assault which saw Stephen sentenced to a few weeks in Darlinghurst Gaol. For his offences over time, the court was more lenient with William and he usually escaped with fines and warnings. In 1859 he got out of the pub and the butcher shop and sold his piggery and pork butchering business as well, at which time he then appears with his wife Martha and his brother Stephen living at the property in Bigga.

Over the next few years, the Benyon's worked their land running cattle and growing crops. It appears also that the house was used as somewhat of an inn.

Following William Benyon's death at the hands of John Peisley in 1862, his wife Martha returned to Sydney where she ran some pubs. Sadly, with what appeared to be financial issues, she literally drank herself to death at the early age of forty one. Stephen went to Queensland where he married, before returning to the butchering trade in Sydney.

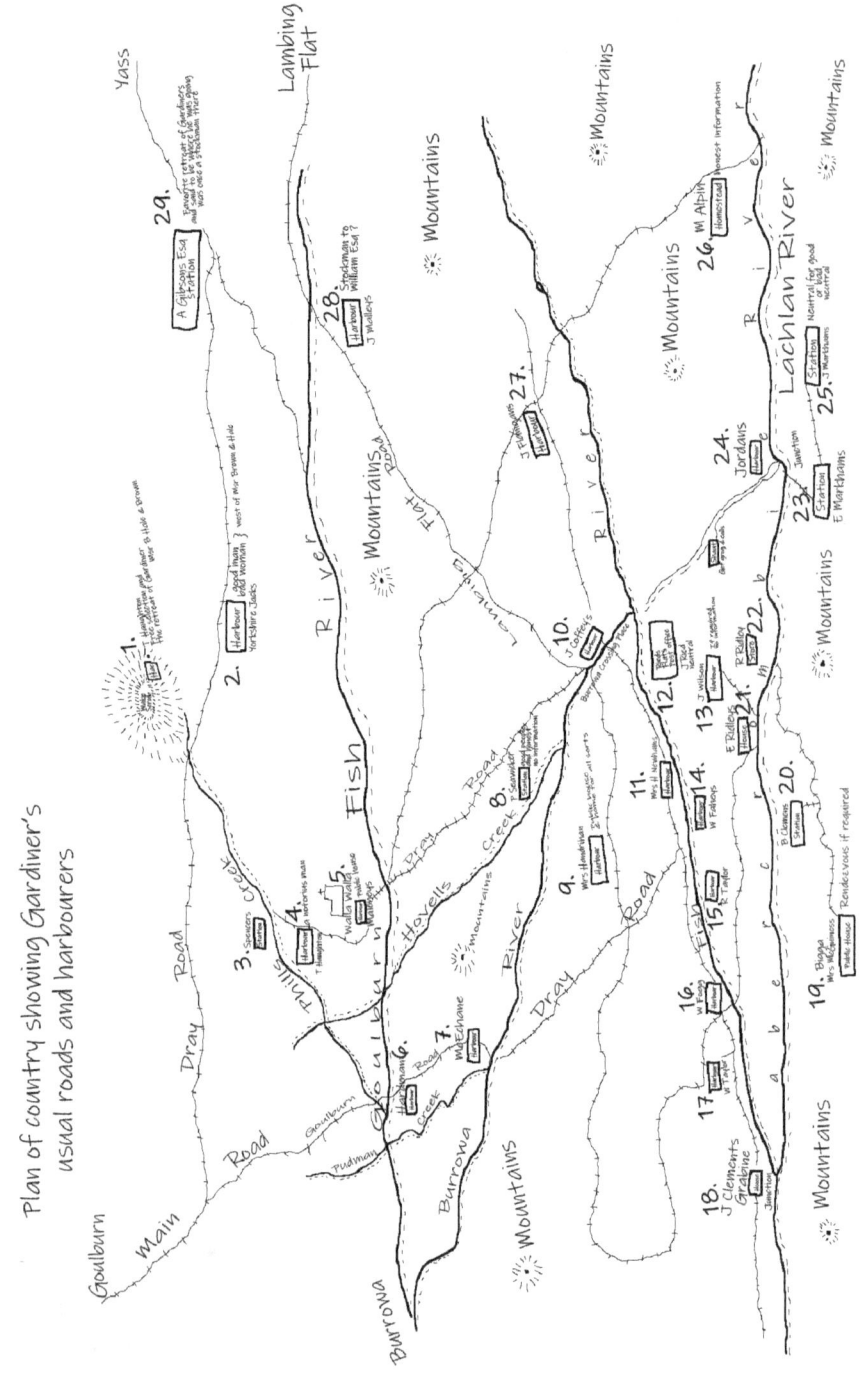

Map index

1. T Haughton - Free selection and the retreat of Gardiner
2. Yorkshire Jacks – harbour – good man and bad woman
3. Spencers - station
4. T Haughton – harbour – a notorious man
5. Maloneys – Walla Walla public house - harbour
6. Hardman - harbour
7. McEchane – harbour
8. P Seawicker – good and honest people, no information
9. Mrs Handriham – harbour – public house & home for all sorts
10. J Coffeys - Harbour
11. Mrs H Newhams - harbour
12. J Ried – Ried's Flat Post Office - neutral
13. J Wilson – harbour – if required no information
14. W Fahyes - harbour
15. R Taylor - harbour
16. W Fogg - harbour
17. W Taylor - harbour
18. J Clemmens - Grabine Junction - Harbourer
19. Mrs McGuiness – Bigga Public House – rendezvous if required
20. B Clemens - station
21. E Ridleys - house
22. R Ridley - store
23. E Markhams - station
24. Jordans - harbour
25. J Markhams – station – neutral for good or bad
26. M Alpin – homestead – honest information
27. J Flanigans - harbour
28. J Malleys - harbour
29. A Gibson Esq – station - Favorite retreat of Gardiners and said to be where he was going, was once a stockman there

Capture

After the shooting of William Benyon, John Peisley was now on the run, more than ever. Now he was also wanted for shooting a man, the reward for his apprehension and conviction was raised to £175. His charges included the murder of Benyon, the attempted murder of Middleton and Hosie and horse stealing. Despite the large reward offered, no-one came forward with information.

The police appeared helpless, or perhaps hapless. In trying to track Peisley down, they faced severe criticism in the press, not limited to their failure to find him but also alluding to the possibility that William Benyon would still be alive if they had. Middleton and Hosie had just been applauded for their actions at Fogg's Hut, with Middleton awarded a silver medal for bravery - so their inability to find and arrest Peisley must have weighed heavily.

By the middle of January 1862, the hunt for Peisley was on in full earnest, throughout the Western regions of New

South Wales, stretching from Cowra to the northwest, Bathurst to the north and Goulburn to the south. At one point, the absence of police at the various watchhouses caused great concern after it was found that no-one was around to sign for prisoners. This included Carcoar's police magistrate, Owen Beardmore, as well as the police magistrates at Bathurst and Cowra. Where were they? Out with the Peisley hunting parties they had ordered. Magistrates hunting their accused man!

Several criminals were released because of not being able to be processed, including one criminal in Bathurst by the name of John Griffiths, who was going by the alias John Peisley.

January 1862

> Since the perpetration of this new outrage, a large body of police from Tuena and Carcoar have been out in search of the criminal. Today, Constables Bunon, Walker, and Morrice set out in pursuit from Goulburn, and it is to be hoped that we shall soon hear of this most dangerous character being in safe custody. It may be added that the settlers out Taralga way are seriously apprehensive of a visit from Peisley, and in one or two cases warnings of such an unwelcome visit have been given. As a proof that such fears are not altogether without some foundation, we may state it is known for a certainty that this now infamous bushranger was actually

at Taralga, within thirty miles of Goulburn, a few days ago.

— The Albury Banner and Wodonga Express, 15 January 1862, page 4

Peisley continued to evade them. He was reported to be in Berrima while simultaneously being seen near Albury. There were reports of him continuing with robberies at Bigga and one report said he was in Sydney. The Western Examiner newspaper reported that Peisley had bailed up the collector of the electoral roll for the Carcoar district, and insisted his name be put down as a voter.

News wasn't limited to New South Wales. Based on rumours, one major Melbourne newspaper reported Peisley dead.

January 1862

PEISLEY THE BUSHRANGER - A rumour was afloat through the town on Friday, to the effect that the notorious Peisley had at last received his quietus. It was reported positively that he was shot, but how, or by whom, we cannot learn. There can be but little doubt that this ruffian has become so hardened (if he be not dead) that there is but little chance of ever taking him alive.

— The Argus, 18 January 1862, page 7

With what appears to be most of the western constabulary out looking for Peisley, over the coming weeks there were near misses.

In late January, Constable Paget from Binda reported that he had been out looking for Peisley for twelve days. He said that on the fifteenth of January, he sighted Peisley and took off after him, but he escaped. Then came the report of the efforts of the police from Goulburn who, while riding toward Bigga, caught up with Peisley riding a "well bred black mare".

After exchanging some words, Peisley confirmed he was the man they were looking for. Constable Morriss told him to get off his horse - Peisley said he would if Morriss laid down his gun, which Morriss did. The story then goes that either one of the troopers secretly handed Morriss a revolver, or that he had a gun concealed beneath his jacket. Peisley claimed to be unarmed and refused to dismount fearing the troopers would rush at him. Morriss said they would not, however Peisley was not persuaded, turned his horse and rode off. Morriss then fired three shots at Peisley, all of which missed.

A week or so later, a corporal saw Peisley at Tarcutta, some two hundred kilometres south of Bigga, judging by the horse he was on and his appearance fitting Peisley's description. He ordered him to stop, then rode up beside him. Holding a pistol to Peisley's head, he asked him to remove his hat, wanting to see if he was bald. Peisley then turned and rode off at full gallop, pursued by the corporal who fired at him, but missed.

Peisley was indeed heading south, likely to Albury where one of his brothers lived, and then possibly onto the goldfields in Victoria. When reporting the Tarcutta encounter, the press believe he was heading for Victoria. Then, the very next day some other police staked out a man camped at Berambula thinking it was Peisley. When the supposed bushranger awoke, he was horrified to himself covered by a brace of pistols. Unfortunately, it was not Peisley.

Condemnation of the police efforts continued.

February 1862

> In the meanwhile we cannot help joining with the Bathurst journals and crying "shame" on the Western Patrol, whose business it specially has been to capture this robber and murderer. Although unsuccessful as yet in the main object of their pursuit, the police have apprehended one Newman, a cattle stealer, and Zhan, a former mate of Peisley's, the last for giving them false information, and thus leading to the inference that he is still in collusion with the murderer of Benyon, who, to the lasting disgrace of the Western Mounted Police and their commandant, is still at large among the Abercrombie ranges. – Goulburn Chronicle
>
> — The Albury Banner and Wodonga Express, 1 February 1862, page 3

Citizen's arrest

Then came the news that everyone had waited for. On Wednesday 29th January 1862, John Peisley was finally caught. However it was not by police, despite them having scoured the district. Peisley was caught by a private citizen.

A very effective rumour had made its way to Mundarlo, just west of Wagga Wagga, that Peisley had evaded capture, but in the process lost his packhorse. A man called Beveridge from Wantabadgerie, visited McKenzie's public house at Tarcutta having heard that a man who lost a packhorse was staying the night.

Planning the capture, Beveridge enlisted the help of the inn owner and one other to take Peisley into custody. At this time Peisley was in the kitchen having a meal. Another man who had been working for Beveridge that day, was lying drunk near the door. Having finished his meal, Peisley then tried to wake the drunken man, who became agitated and challenged Peisley to fight for £1, but Peisley refused. Beveridge and his collaborators were listening to their conversation and later said they had hoped a fight would ensue as they figured that would have been a good opportunity to take Peisley.

When the fight didn't eventuate, Beveridge and his men then grabbed Peisley while he was lifting a cup of tea to his mouth, winding his arms to his back, and reaching to disarm him. McKenzie then handcuffed him and Peisley was thus secured.

Gundagai

With Gundagai being the nearest lockup to Tarcutta, Peisley was transferred there to be formally processed by the police bench. With his identity determined, he was then sent to Carcoar to "undergo examination on a charge of having murderously assaulted troopers Hosie and Middleton." On the way to Carcoar under a strong escort consisting of six mounted men, including the chief-constable of Gundagai, he was held overnight at the lockup in Burrowa. Here he was handed over to the solitary policeman at the temporary police quarters who, feeling compassion, took the handcuffs off Peisley for a minute or two. Seizing opportunity, Peisley then bolted and got away. He was not, however, many minutes in the enjoyment of freedom when he was recaptured.

Carcoar

On Wednesday 12th February 1862, John Peisley was bought to the Carcoar courthouse to face committal proceedings. His charge was the wilful murder of William Benyon and the courthouse was packed with spectators. Notably the charge of supposedly assaulting Middleton and Hosie was missing. As was the horse stealing. It's probable these were never pursued in court as they figured they had Peisley for the straight up murder of Benyon.

The presiding magistrate was a familiar face - Owen Beardmore. The rest of the bench were also no strangers to John Peisley - Connely, North, Meyer, and Lynch.

Seven witnesses were called and recounted their experiences of the events at the Benyon home, which led to William Benyon's eventual death. Peisley remained cool, if not unconcerned. Convinced the police had a case, he was then fully committed for trial at Bathurst.

Bathurst

Peisley's next appearance was at Bathurst Gaol, arriving with an escort of no less than nine mounted troopers, all armed with revolvers. He was led to the gaol on a horse, mounted with his hands cuffed to the pummel of the saddle. By this time a crowd had gathered at the gaol to catch a glimpse of the man that had so long evaded capture. In many reports, the attitude of the crowd was described as depressed, showing maudlin expressions, with the observation made that many would have been glad to have seen him set free.

The gaoler then read his charges and said that despite his grave offenses, he would be treated the same as all other prisoners. By accounts, Peisley was well behaved, if not even cheerful. When later spoken to about his crime of murder, he appeared sorrowful, but quickly shook that off, saying that it was too late to alter the case, and useless to lament it.

Despite the fact the notorious Peisley was now firmly behind bars, the press' relentless criticism of the police authorities continued. When Peisley was being transferred to Carcoar, they wrote:

February 1862

We shall be much surprised if the escort succeeds in safely landing Peisley at Carcoar. We consider the authorities at Gundagai much to blame in ordering so dangerous a character as Peisley to be escorted direct to Carcoar, as he would have to pass through a country infested at the present time with bushrangers, who would no doubt willingly lend a hand for his rescue. Peisley has a thorough knowledge of the whole of that part of the district, and has, no doubt, many confederates located in the quarter who would facilitate his escape. As there is a charge of murder against this desperado, it would have been a more judicious plan to have had him conveyed straight to Goulburn - the Abercrombie, where Benyon was murdered, being within the limits of that police district; and there would have been no hardship, even if it were not, to have compelled the attendance of witnesses there. The main southern road, with its lockups and police patrol, would have afforded a more secure route than the cross-country one.

— The Golden Age (Queanbeyan),
13 February 1862, page 2

Sold the road

RIGHT OF BUSHRANGING.—Mr Peisley may certainly be considered one of the most daring and impudent bushrangers who have ever infested the colony of New South Wales, and it seems that he was so held among the honourable fraternity to which he belongs, as the following anecdote will prove. It seems while he was recently in the Gundagai lockup, he fell across another gentleman in difficulties, who informed him that he had himself been stuck up on the Southern road, adding, "I don't think it was you who did it though." "No, no," replied Mr Peisley, "I sold the right of that road five years ago, so it's not likely I should have stuck you up." We have heard of selling a milk-walk or a crossing sweeping, but we never expected to hear of a man disposing of a branch bushranging business, doubtless a very profitable one, although not in every respect desirable.—*Wagga Wagga Express*.

Bell's Life in Sydney and Sporting Chronicle, 15 March 1862, page 2

Trial

On 10th March 1862, Justice Edward Wise entered the Circuit Court at Bathurst to preside over the trial of John Peisley for the murder of William Benyon. Again the court was packed with excited spectators. The judge read the charge, that Peisley "on the 28th day of December 1861 at Bigga in the County of Bathurst, in the colony of New South Wales, did feloniously, wilfully, and of his malice aforethought kill and murder one William Benyon." Calm and collected, Peisley pleaded in a firm voice – "Not guilty".

The Judge then acknowledged that he had received Peisley's application for counsel to be appointed, but then refused the request. In 1862, prisoners were not entitled to legal aid and the appointment of a defence Counsel was at the discretion of the judge, regardless of whether it was a capital crime or not. In country areas, including Bathurst, it was considered too costly for barristers to be expected to travel from Sydney without payment, so defendants were expected to either pay for a barrister or defend themselves, even in the case of murder charges that could result in a death sentence. Only aboriginal prisoners were to be granted Counsel regardless of their circumstances, at the Government's expense.

Peisley then stated that he had two horses, that if the Judge would permit to be sold, would raise funds sufficient to cover the cost of Counsel. The Judge agreed and adjourned the case for two days.

This point is interesting in that Peisley must have been gifted the horses, as he was stripped of all of his belongings at the Gundagai Police lockup. They had been sold by the Gundagai police a few weeks earlier.

> THE undermentioned property, found in possession of John Peisley, is now in custody of the Police at Gundagai, and will be sold by public auction, at 1 o'clock, on Thursday, 27th February, 1862, viz. :—
>
> 1 bay horse, branded ſI (the ſ reversed) near shoulder, large flesh lump under.
> 1 saddle
> 1 pair of red blankets
> 1 pair of Blucher boots
> 3 regatta shirts
> 2 Crimean shirts
> 1 old pilot coat
> 1 pair of trousers
> 1 waistcoat
> 1 blue shirt
> 1 bell
> 2 turnscrews
> 1 black silk necktie
> 3 old silk handkerchiefs
> 2 cotton handkerchiefs
> 1 pair of cotton socks.
>
> By order of Police Magistrate,
> JAMES ST. CLAIR,
> Chief Constable.
>
> Police Office, Gundagai,
> 15th February, 1862.

New South Wales Government Gazette, 25 February 1862 (issue no 45), page 453

When the trial recommenced on March 13th, Peisley had retained Arthur Holroyd to defend him, and on opening the case, the Acting Attorney General representing the crown reminded the jury to ignore everything they had heard prior to this case coming to court.

They were reminded that Benyon and Peisley were known to each other and that a quarrel had taken place on 27th December at Benyon's house involving a horse trade some seventeen years earlier, and that a fight ensued. The jury was told that if drinking had not been involved, the horse trade probably would not have been remembered. They were told that following interference in the fight by Stephen Benyon which included Peisley being hit in the head with a shovel, Peisley had threatened him.

When Peisley then left for Bigga to get a new shirt, Stephen Benyon returned to work in the barn and was armed with a double barrelled gun, preparing for Peisley to come back. The jury was told that it was the events that happened after Peisley came back that they would have to form an opinion as to whether the acts he performed were, or were not, the acts of a man who did not know what he was doing, or whether they were done by design. They were told that Peisley may have been so drunk that he didn't know what he was doing, but the Judge would them remind them that drunkenness was no excuse for crime.

Upon Peisley's return to the farm, he tried to make friends with Stephen Benyon, but then snatched the double barrelled gun and threatened Stephen Benyon, resulting in Benyon being shot in the arm. Peisley then threatened another man working with Stephen, causing the second barrel of the gun to go off accidentally.

Hearing the gunfire, William Benyon left his house and went to the barn. He then got into a fight with Peisley and it was at this point he was shot by Peisley with a revolver. It was this shot that led to the eventual death of William Benyon.

The Attorney General then said that all the expressions used by Peisley, given the circumstances, it was apparent that all Peisley did was by design. This meant he was acting with malice and intent.

He then told the jury that "the facts of the case were so revolting and horrible that one could scarcely be induced to believe that human nature could be so thoroughly depraved, and anyone who would destroy life under such circumstances must be guilty of murder." He went on to say that if any man kills another, the law supposed the existence of malice and that it was up to the accused person to prove otherwise, such to reduce the case to manslaughter or justifiable homicide. He said his knowledge of the case, there was "not a single incident in the whole affair" which would see Peisley's crime reduced to manslaughter.

Following the opening, one by one the witnesses were called up to give their testimony, this time able to be cross examined by John Peisley's defence Counsel, Arthur Holroyd

Thomas McGuiness junior recounted the events that took place at his father's public house and at his home, which did not differ with the testimony given at the committal trial. However, part of his testimony included the night before the day in question, where Peisley and Wilson had drunk six or seven glasses of wine. The following morning they had taken a bottle of wine and a bottle of brandy (or rum) with them when they left for Benyon's farm. He stated that when he returned to his farm for a new shirt, Peisley was more than half drunk. He reiterated that Peisley said he was returning to Benyon's farm to "wing" Stephen Benyon.

Martha Benyon's testimony also did not differ from the committal. The fight with her husband William Benyon happened, Peisley's guns were hidden, Stephen Benyon did get involved. She also stated that her maid told William Benyon where the guns were hidden and that he insisted she give them back to Peisley.

She said drinking at lunch (before any shooting) consisted of two bottles of wine and ale. Martha Benyon was not a witness to Peisley later shooting her husband. She claimed Peisley was sober when he was later at the barn and that she was very frightened the whole time he was there. She stated that despite several people, including possibly ten farmhands, being present at the time of the shooting, nobody made any attempt to detain Peisley. She denied hearing Peisley say to her husband "…you have only yourself to blame. If you had not rushed on me, I should not have shot you."

A farmhand named George Harmer, and James Wilson also took the stand, repeating their versions of events. Then it was the turn of the maid, Mary Ann Samson. She recounted the lunch had with William in the house, the hiding of the guns and the episode with the shirt. She also said that when his pistols were returned to him, Peisley said "I am alright now" and that William Benyon asked if Peisley was going to shoot him, that Peisley replied "I never did a cowardly action". In her testimony she said that Peisley threatened to "put a bullet through the heart" of Stephen Benyon and that he held both Stephen and James Wilson at gunpoint. She also said that Peisley threatened to shoot her.

Mary Ann testified that she was present in the barn when Peisley shot Stephen Benyon and when he later shot William Benyon. After shooting William, Peisley said to her "is the bastard dead? If not I'll put a ball through his brain." When she exclaimed "oh my poor master", Peisley said "I know what I am doing."

Under cross-examination by Holroyd, Mary Ann testified that she was still living with Martha Benyon and that they had often talked about the affair. After confirming the fights with the Benyons again, she testified that she did not think that Peisley was drunk.

Then she was questioned about Martha Benyon and Jane Wilson, to which she testified that she did not recall saying that she would do whatever she could to see Peisley hanged.

Stephen Benyon then called to the stand recounted his version of events without adding anything different to the committal hearing, or other witnesses. He did not witness Peisley shooting his brother. Another witness who saw Stephen Benyon hit Peisley on the head with a shovel, causing Peisley to be stunned and drop a knife he was carrying. He stated he thought Peisley was very drunk.

Martha Benyon was recalled to answer questions about her exchanges with Jane Wilson – the wife of James Wilson. She admitted that she'd had some conversations with Jane while on the road to Bathurst for the court hearings and that they talked about the weather. She stated that Jane Wilson had not said to her "this is a bad job about Peisley. I don't think he'll be hanged." Martha then denied having said to Jane "wait till I get to the court, I'll have the wretch hanged if I can."

For the defence, Holroyd then recalled Jane Wilson who testified that Martha Benyon was determined to see Peisley hanged. Her statement – "I am the wife of James Wilson; coming from Bigga to Bathurst I saw Mrs Benyon on the road. I said it was a bad job about Peisley but I did not think he would be hanged, he would get a long sentence." Martha Benyon then said, when she got to court she would see what she would do, she would hang the wretch if she could.

In closing the defence, Holroyd addressed the jury stating that while William Benyon did die from wounds inflicted by Peisley, it followed that the wounds had not been inflicted with malice or forethought. When the prisoner saw Benyon rushing him, he might have thought that he wanted to get possession of his pistols and that his own life would be in danger, in which case he would only be defending himself.

There were three points to be considered by the jury. Was the act one of wilful and premeditated murder ? Was the shooting accidental ? Or did Peisley believe his own life was in danger and therefore fired in self defence? Holroyd then asked the jury to consider if, at the time, Peisley was in such a state as to be able to distinguish between right and wrong. And as his life depended upon their decision, he hoped they would give a most careful consideration and arrive at a correct conclusion.

In closing for the Crown, Butler spoke in forcible terms of the state of the Abercrombie district where Peisley had so long been allowed to go at large. He stated that people of the neighbourhood were associating with him even though they knew he was living in open violation of the law. He argued that even if Holroyd's law was correct there was not the slightest ground for supposing that Peisley, at the time he shot Benyon, was incapable of distinguishing between right and wrong. Referring to the suggestion that Peisley possibly acted in self defence, he reminded the jury that Peisley had already violated the law and therefore, had anyone rushed him, with the view of disarming him or securing him, had been shot, such shooting would be murder.

The jury then adjourned but it did not take them long to consider. Ten minutes later they returned to the court with a verdict of guilty.

The spectators in the court erupted and the Judge called for silence. He then asked John Peisley if he had anything to say and why the sentence of death should not be passed upon him. Peisley replied that he did not deny shooting Benyon, but that he did not intend to kill him – his only dispute with him related to a horse swap.

The Judge then pronounced the sentence of death.

News reports noted that Peisley's demeanour during the whole trial was quiet, almost disinterested. When his sentence was proclaimed he tried to talk to the jury saying "As a jury of my country have found me guilty…" but the Judge ordered him removed from the court. When he was taken outside to return to the gaol, a large crowd had gathered. One of Peisley's friends yelled at him "well Johnny, what is it?", to which Peisley replied "Oh, it's a swinger."

Hanged man

John Peisley's execution by hanging was set for the morning of Friday 25th April 1862. Overnight, residents had reported feeling and hearing the rumble of an earthquake in the district and the weather for that day was described as gloomy with storm clouds threatening.

At exactly 9 am, Peisley was led from his cell at the Bathurst gaol, wearing chains, his head shaved. Two clergymen accompanied him through the corridors, walking toward the gallows where about fifty people had gathered as spectators to his death. The clergymen read from their bibles, quoting the Christian funeral service as they walked. After kneeling for prayer at the foot of the gallows, they then ascended to the awaiting scaffold. Peisley then turned to the crowd that faced him.

He said he appeared before them at the point of his death, charged with the crime of wilful murder and that if any man were guilty of committing such a murder as had been represented at his trial, he would justly deserve to die. He said that he did not deny for a moment that William Benyon had died because of his actions, then stated that the circumstances had not been truly told during his trial, and that if they had, he may not be facing the gallows.

He then described his personal version of the events at Benyon's house – having not had the opportunity to do so during his trial. He said he went to Benyon's because he had been told by Tom McGuiness that Benyon wanted to see him, intimating that his reason for going there in the first place was not to murder Benyon. Upon reaching Benyon's house, with his friend James Wilson in tow, the group including Benyon spent some time drinking "grog".

He then said that Benyon asked him to sing and dance, which he said he could not, so Benyon then asked him to put gloves on and fight. Peisley said no, saying this would end in a row.

At this point one of the clergymen had a word in Peisley's ear, interrupting his speech, to which Peisley said he would say nothing further on that matter, but continued his speech.

He said he had been represented as a bushranger and an outrageous character. He admitted that he had violated laws, but he looked upon himself as the most honourable bushranger. He said he had never used any violence to, or taken a shilling from a woman, and there were several ladies in Bathurst who could testify as to the treatment they had received from him.

Although he had been charged with many crimes of which he had not the slightest knowledge, he begged to assure them that he had never, until the affair at Benyon's, been guilty of using violence to man, woman, or child.

He then spoke about the charge made against him concerning the rescue of Gardiner from Sergeant Middleton and Trooper Hosie at Fogg's Hut. He called God to witness, that the charge was groundless, that he was not anywhere near the spot claimed by Trooper Hosie.

Then his speech delved into what he believe happened at Foggs. He said he was aware that Fogg had promised Trooper Hosie £50 if he would let Gardiner go free. Hosie agreed and paid Hosie the sum of £50. Among the money paid to Hosie, was a cheque for £2 10s, and that was the reason of his receiving ten shillings over the £50.

Continuing, he said that some "evil" person had caused to be published in the newspapers, an article intimating that he had robbed and severely ill-treated a woman at the General's Gap. That charge was also false, as he did not know anything this.

He concluded his speech saying that he hoped God would forgive all his enemies, as he forgave them freely and fully. His last words were "Good bye gentlemen, and God bless you."

With this the fatal rope was then adjusted and a white cap was drawn over his face. By a signal from the Acting-Sheriff, the floor was then released, and Peisley fell to his death.

At the same time, the aboriginal Jackie Bullfrog, also convicted of murder, stood beside Peisley awaiting his own death. While Peisley did not appear to suffer much nor long, Bullfrog convulsed for several minutes before finally hanging limp. After hanging the usual time both bodies were cut down, and being placed in coffins were convoyed to their last resting place.

Reaction

In the weeks following Peisley's sentencing a few extraordinary things happened. Despite the endless press reports saying the community had lived in constant terror of Peisley and his cohorts, the community responded with petitions for the Crown to show mercy and spare his life. The petitions were numerous and came from as far east as Sydney:

April 1862

> EXECUTIONS AT BATHURST - Great influence has been brought to bear in favour of Peisley, and numerous petitions have been sent into the Executive from parties never before known to interest themselves in matters of this nature, but we believe wholly without effect as the Government have decided that it is not a case calling for the exercise of mercy, and

> they have determined not to interpose on his behalf, and his execution will, therefore, take place at an early date.
>
> -- Bathurst Free Press and Mining Journal, 19 April 1862, page 2

April 1862

> Great exertions were made to obtain a reprieve for Peisley. Memorials from Bathurst and others from Sydney and the suburbs, being forwarded to the Executive even up to Wednesday. His Honor Mr Justice Wise, who tried the prisoner, however, declined to recommend a mitigation of the sentence and the Executive decided that the law take its course.
>
> -- Bell's Life in Sydney and Sporting Chronicle, 26 April 1862, page 2

One petition (still in existence) emanated from Tambaroora, a tiny village to the north of Hill End in New South Wales. Peisley's brother Benjamin was among a small community of miners there. They called for clemency, the petition signed by nearly one hundred and thirty residents and making up almost the entire population. (A copy of the petition is held by the Hill End & Tambaroora Gathering Group.)

The press were less sympathetic, with some news reports calling for his death being used as a deterrent for crimes, that coincidentally had not decreased since Peisley's capture.

April 1862

> The exact time for the execution of the above prisoners [Peisley and Bullfrog], we have been unable to learn, that it is understood that the executioner will visit Bathurst before proceeding to Goulburn. It is many years since so many persons have been under sentence of death in this colony at one time, and it is to be hoped that the decision arrived at by the Executive to carry out the sentence of the law to the last extremity, will have the effect of deterring some of the misguided men who are at present committing robberies and outrage in the Western and Southern districts from a further course of crime.
>
> -- Empire, 17 April 1862, page 4

The crimes did not subside. All the petitions were to no avail.

Notably, as John Peisley never faced the court on either the charge of horse stealing or the affair at Fogg's Hut, while present, Middleton and Hosie did not have to participate in the trial. Presumably, once Peisley was found guilty of the murder of Benyon, the other charges became irrelevant.

Memoirs

The second event that is mentionable is the release of memoirs, issued prior to his hanging. It took less than one week for some individuals to capitalise on Peisley's plight. Several memoirs were published and widely advertised for sale.

> **PEISLEY.**
>
> **Published This Day, Price 6d., by Post 9d.,**
>
> A BRIEF MEMOIR OF JOHN PEISLEY,
>
> With a Full Report of his Trial and Condemnation for the Murder of WILLIAM BENYON.
>
> Sold by A. K. THOMSON, and all Booksellers.

Advertisement - Bathurst Free Press and Mining Journal, 26 March 1862, page 3 (a copy of this memoir is held at the New South Wales State Library as part of the Justice Wise collection).

> WILL be PUBLISHED, on WEDNESDAY MORNING, the "The Trial of John Peisley, for the Wilful Murder of John Benyon, with an account of his Life and Bushranging Exploits." Price, Sixpence. To be had of ALLAN and WIGLEY, 297, George-street.

Advertisement, The Sydney Morning Herald, 18 March 1862, page 8

Neither of the above publications have an attributed author, but the Memoir is believed to be a collaboration between two former journalists of the Bathurst Free Press and Bathurst Times. The Memoir details some of Peisley's early history and has a lengthy account of the trial. The latter part is dedicated to the morality of John Peisley stating that he and other bushrangers were "…living in a state of practical heathenism, as far removed from accepted ideas of civilized and Christian existence as the darkness of midnight from the glare of the noon-day sun."

The Memoir then finishes with a detailed and quite complimentary physical description of John Peisley, and then perhaps something more telling of the day, showing the absence of understanding about the psychology of the criminal mind in the 1860s. It concludes with an observation that "part of the head assigned by phrenologists to the seat of the moral organs is very small compared to the size of the lateral portion of the cranium, and would give rise to the idea that, when once his animal passions and propensities were aroused, his moral capabilities would be altogether insufficient to counterbalance their destructive tendencies." Fortunately, both society and science have moved forward since then.

Bullfrog

It was a busy week at the Bathurst Assizes with the Judge hearing, along with assorted other crimes, seven cases of murder with intent to kill. Of those cases, two men found guilty joined the line of those sentenced to death in New South Wales. In the same week the Goulburn Court heard several cases involving murder with intent, resulting in another five men being sentenced to death.

The day following John Peisley's guilty verdict, another Bathurst inhabitant was indicted for murder. His name was Jackey Bullfrog (alias Flash Jack) and he was an aborigine. He was described as very intelligent, spoke English fluently and appeared to be quite aware of the proceedings and the position he was in.

Bullfrog stood trial for having wilfully murdered a man he encountered trying to cross a river. Bullfrog was carrying a spear, a wommera and a boomerang. He robbed the man and killed him with the spear, although it was contested that it was his mate that did the murder with a tomahawk. Nonetheless, like Peisley before him, the jury found him guilty and he was also sentenced to death. His case is noted from the guilty verdicts handed down that week as he was to face the gallows on the same day as Peisley.

Included in the court lists were a string of cases involving everything from robbery under arms, forgery, assault and rape. Of those found guilty the penalties ranged from three to ten years of hard labour.

Of those condemned to death at Goulburn, three went to the gallows, with two sentences commuted to fifteen years hard labour. April 1862 was to become a murderous month, sending a strong message to those who broke the law. Despite the heavy sentences handed down, the reports of bushranging continued, unabated.

Aftermath

Middleton and Hosie

John Peisley's dying words regarding Sergeant Middleton and Trooper Hosie would come to haunt both of the policemen.

Just weeks after John Peisley's arrest and only a few days before his trial, Trooper William Hosie was promoted to Constable in the Western District (H Division) of New South Wales as part of the New Police Regulation Act which came into force in March 1862. Then in June – two months later, Hosie was sacked from the New South Wales Police Force. He was also fined £2. The coincidence of the fine did not go unnoticed.

June 1862

Trooper Wm Hosie — It will be recollected that some months ago troopers Middleton and Hosie had an encounter with the noted bushrangers, Gardiner and Peisley, and both of them were wounded in the affray, Middleton severely. Considerable praise was awarded to the troopers at the time, a subscription being also raised for them, although they did not succeed in securing the highwaymen. It has lately been rumoured, on strength of a statement made by Peisley on the scaffold, that a man named Fogg, some how connected with the bushrangers, gave Hosie £50 to let Gardiner escape. We are not aware what truth there was in the statement, but we observe by the Police Gazette of the 11th inst. that Hosie has been dismissed from the force, and that he had also been fined £2. The offence is not mentioned. — Goulburn Herald.

— The Yass Courier,
21 June 1862, page 3

> **FINES.**
> Mounted Const. Wm. Hosie, £2.
>
> **DISMISSED.**
> Mounted Const. Wm. Hosie, from 4th instant.

New South Wales Police Gazette and Weekly
Record of Crime, 11 June 1862, page 89

In June 1864, Hosie was no longer a policeman, however he testified at the trial of Frank Gardiner who faced the court accused of the intent to murder Middleton and Hosie at Fogg's Hut.

When cross-examined about the claim Peisley had freed Gardiner, Hosie repeated that Peisley had aimed a pistol at him while ordering him to let Gardiner go free. He knew that Peisley had since been executed and admitted he had last seen Peisley when he was being held in Bathurst Gaol. He then went on to state that Peisley was not tried for anything connected with rescue of Gardiner.

When asked directly whether he had taken a bribe, his defence attorney objected to the question and Hosie was not required to answer. He (Hosie) did not "renew" the Gardiner escape charge when Peisley was in custody and noted again that Peisley was not brought up upon such a charge. He finished by stating that in his testimony, he had not omitted anything of importance that took place with his interview with Peisley. He never admitted to having taken a bribe, or having erroneously or perhaps feloniously dumped Peisley's name right in it.

Middleton also ran foul. In May 1863 he was transferred from Tuena to Orange, then a few months later he was demoted from sergeant to constable. In January 1864, prior to Frank Gardiner's trial, he resigned from the police force.

The Eugowra Gold Robbery

It was hoped that Peisley's death would somehow set an example for other would be bushrangers, however this was not the case. Robberies on the roads around the plains of Western New South Wales continued to make the news daily. The deeds were the same, only the names had changed.

Six weeks after Peisley's hanging, the single largest gold robbery in Australian history took place at Eugowra, west of Bathurst.

On Sunday 15th June 1862, a gang of bushrangers led by Frank Gardiner held up the Lachlan Gold Escort at Escort Rock, some five kilometres east of Eugowra. The members of Gardiner's gang were identified as Johnny Gilbert, John Bow, Alex Fordyce, Henry Manns (alias Turner), Dan Charters, Ben Hall, and John O'Meally. This famous robbery netted Gardiner and his gang £14,000 of gold and cash. In today's money (2024) this would be worth between $6 million and $10 million. The significance of this robbery catapulted many of the gang, such as Ben Hall and Johhny Gilbert, including Gardiner into Australian history fame, and eventually lead to their untimely deaths.

Epitaph

There is no doubt that John Peisley was a scoundrel. There is no denying that he caused the death of William Benyon, however it remains debateable as to whether this was murder with intent, or manslaughter, but for this he will be remembered, and much of what is written about him will focus on this fact alone.

What is evident though is this: given his history, John Peisley was never going to be able to lead the life of what we would term today, a good upstanding citizen. From his very early beginnings, he had unsettled role models – his convict father in gaol, his convict mother taken off with a man of dubious origins. He was for all intents left alone in the bush to fend for himself at a very young age. His family split in every direction.

There were many influential people around him that had reason to see him fail. His wealthy neighbour Icely who was no doubt happy to see the entire Peisley family off "his" land. The police magistrate Owen Beardmore, who had everything to gain by appeasing the wealthy and setting examples. The local police officers who needed to cement their positions in the face of changing regulations. The police force in general who had to fend off the constant criticism of their ability to curtail crime and apprehend criminals in Western New South Wales.

And then there were the journalists who fed their columns with Peisley's antics, demonising him at every chance and attaching his name to almost every crime, often without any evidence, justified or not.

His supposed friends and social circles did him no favours either. The murder of Benyon was reported by Martha Benyon, who had a death to avenge, finding Peisley a worthy scapegoat. The affair at Fogg's Hut bandied his name by almost everyone involved. Nobody stood up for him at any point.

From aged nineteen, till his execution just nine years later, John Peisley's "schooling" had been from incarceration in many of New South Wales's most notorious prisons – Bathurst Gaol, Darlinghurst Gaol, Goulburn Gaol and Cockatoo Island, all of which had been described as existing in the most depraved of conditions. Here he associated with many similar criminals – from robbers to hardened murderers, all no doubt teaching him the tools of their trades. His role models were dubious, his fate inevitable.

For John Peisley his future, rather than being described as a life of crime, could easily be transposed as the crime of life, and that life was extinguished when he was just twenty eight years of age.

Other info

The following is provided as a guide only for future family research and represents information available at the time of publication. Where information has not been confirmed by an original and official record source such as a birth certificate, obituary or will etc, the letter "U" indicates it is unconfirmed. Acknowledgement is made to all those dedicated to researching this family and the hope that we can all refine information as research progresses.

Sarah Green

1788 – born in Cripplegate, Middlesex, England

1788 Apr 6 – Baptised at St Giles Church of England, Cripplegate, London

1811 Jun 17 – living at 32 Marleybone Lane, London, the servant of William Liddiard

1811 (U) – possible marriage to Matthew Clayton, however unlikely due to her incarceration at the time. No record of a marriage could be found.

1812 Jun 4 - The ship "Indefatigable" sailed from England on meeting up with the ship "Minstrel" on 29 July 1812 in Rio de Janeiro (Brazil). The Indefatigable then sailed to Hobart, and the Minstrel to Sydney. Sarah was using the last name Clayton but travelled as Sarah Green.

Justice Hall, in the Old Bailey,

On WEDNESDAY the 18th of SEPTEMBER, 1811, and following Days;

630. SARAH GREEN was indicted for feloniously stealing on the 17th of June, a watch, value 20l. three neckcloths, value 12s. a shawl, value 5s. and seven yards of lace, value 10s. the property of James Cranbourn Strode, in the dwelling house of William Liddiard.

JAMES CRANBOURN STRODE. I am a lodger in the dwelling house of William Liddiard, the prisoner was a servant there, she had access to my lodging.
Q. Did you lose any property—A. I lost a gold repeating watch, a seal, three neck handkerchiefs, and about seven or eight yards of lace.
Q. Did the prisoner leave the house—A. Not upon taking of my things.

WILLIAM JACKSON. I am an officer of Marlborough-street, I apprehended the prisoner at her mother's, Kew Green; this shawl and the coral necklace belonging to Mr. Lidiard, she had in her pocket.
Q. That is not in this indictment—A. I went with the prisoner to her lodgings, 32, Mary-le-bone-lane, there I searched her box in her presence, I found a duplicate of a gold repeater, eight yards of lace, and three muslin handkerchiefs in her box; the prisoner said she knew nothing about it, and was very willing to be searched.

MR. EWER. I am a pawnbroker. I produce a gold watch, I believe it to be pledged by the prisoner. I have very little doubt, but I cannot be positive.

Prosecutor. This is my watch, I know it by the striking of it. This shawl is mine, there is a great deal of work upon it; I know it by the work, and the neckcloths are marked.

The prisoner said nothing in her defence, nor called any witnesses to character.

GUILTY—DEATH, aged 23.

First Middlesex Jury, before Mr. Justice Heath.

According to the death certificate of daughter Elizabeth, Matthew Clayton was a ship's carpenter. For her daughter Elizabeth to been born at sea, Sarah must have been heavily pregnant when she boarded the Minstrel. She was incarcerated in September 1811 (trial sentence) and sailed for Australia in June 1812 which is 9 months. Did she became pregnant while still in prison awaiting transportation? Elizabeth was reportedly born at Sulawesi Tengah, Indonesia on board the Ship "Minstrel" sometime between 11 August 1812 (Minstrel arrived in Rio) and 25 October 1812 (Minstrel arrived in Sydney). This would mean that Sarah became pregnant while incarcerated at the Old Bailey. At the Old Bailey with a death sentence, she would have been in isolation, or at the very least only with female inmates. The only likely scenario is that after Sarah's death sentence was commuted to transportation (life), she was possibly removed from the Old Bailey (Middlesex Gaol) onto a prison hulk sometime between Sep 1811 and Jun 1812. That was common. Matthew may have been a hand on such a hulk.

1812 Oct 25 – arrival in Sydney, New South Wales.

1818 – granted a Ticket of leave, consigned to work in public factory

1819 Sep 26 – Granted permission to marry Matthew Buckley at Castlereagh, New South Wales.

1825/28 – Residing at Nepean or Penrith, New South Wales, as wife of Matthew Buckley on a 14 acre farm called Appledons on the Nepean River.

1835 Aug 15 - Pardoned

1844 Nov 22 – died aged 56 at a Benevolent Asylum in Sydney, New South Wales. A service was held St Lawrence, Church of England.

Thomas Peisley (Peasland)

1797 - born in Alderton, Northamptonshire, England

1799 May 26 – baptised in Alderton, Northamptonshire, England

1819 Oct 5 – held on the Bellerophon Prison Hulk for the crime of highway robbery. His occupation at the time was Farmers Man.

1820 Apr 22 – transported to Australia aboard "Agamemnon", arriving in Sydney 1820 Sep 22. Term 7 years.

1822 Feb 18 – convicted at Liverpool Magistrates Bench for refusing to work. To be sent to the Northern Settlements at Port Macquarie.

1822 Mar 22 – transported to Newcastle among 57 prisoners aboard the HM schooner "Elizabeth Henrietta".

1824 Oct 16 - Sentenced before the Bench of Magistrates, Parramatta for harbouring bushrangers and refusing to assist with their apprehension. He received 25 lashes and was then attached to Rev'd Samuel Marsden's clearing gang. Marsden was a prolific sheep farmer, also known for his brutal treatment of his workers.

1826 Dec 21 – as Thomas Peasland, he received a Certificate of Freedom.

1830 Jan 25 – as Thomas Peasland, he married Elizabeth Clayton by Banns at St James Church, Sydney.

1837 Jun and 1838 Jun – as Thomas Peisley, was recorded as the lessee of land at Rocky Creek River, New South Wales in the area now known as Peisley Creek.

1839 Jul 1 – made an application for 100 acres of land at Neville, however the application was not allowed.

1848 Feb 23 – at the Bathurst Court, Thomas Peisley was found guilty of having stolen a valuable Durham bull calf from his notably wealthy neighbour, Thomas Icely, a landowner, Justice of the Peace, and MP candidate.

1848 – The day following his trial, Thomas Peisley was sentenced to 7 years hard labour.

1848 Mar 14 - Enters Darlinghurst Gaol then to sent to Cockatoo Island.

1848 May 3 – The Peisley cattle, around 500 head, located at Carcoar were sold at auction in Sydney, with the proceeds forfeited to the Crown.

1851 Feb 11 - Convict classification changed class 2 in A division. This allowed him to possibly work for his freedom.

1851 Sep 27 – granted a Ticket of leave to remain in the district of Yass.

Place and date of death is unknown.

Elizabeth Clayton

1812 – born at sea on board the Ship "Minstrel" while her mother was being transported to Australia.

1812 Oct 25 – arrived in Sydney. As she was born of a convict, Elizabeth was classed as a convict on arrival to Australia.

1828 – residing with mother Sarah and step father Matthew Buckley at Penrith at the 14 acre farm called Appledons on the Nepean River. Note this record states the religion of Sarah and Elizabeth as Catholic.

1830 Jan 25 - married Thomas Francis Peasland at St James Church of England in Sydney by Banns.

1848 Apr 18 – letter written to the Sydney Morning Herald in support of her husband Thomas's sentence.

1848/49 – Marriage to George Wilson at Little Forrest, Carcoar, New South Wales. While no official marriage record could be found, her death certificate indicates they were married around 1848-1849. Some research suggests this was in May 1848 – the month following the incarceration of Thomas Peisley.

1856 Oct 29 – She died as Elizabeth Wilson 8 days after giving birth to baby Robert at Bathurst, New South Wales. The baby also died. Her death certificate, as witnessed by her son-in-law Owen Drady, only lists the children she bore with George Wilson.

Children born with Matthew Clayton

Sarah – b 1830 at sea, m John Richards in 1846, m Joseph Bailey in 1875, d 1904 at Rocky Bridge Creek, buried at Neville Cemetery

Children born with Thomas Peisley

Elizabeth – b 1832 at Bathurst, m Owen Drady in 1849 at Carcoar, d 1892 at Carcoar, buried Lyndhurst Cemetery

John – b 1834 at Bathurst, d 1862 at Bathurst, burial place unknown

Anne (U) – b 1836 at Cooming Park Carcoar, d 1926 at Greenmantle or Bigga, buried at Bathurst

Benjamin – b 1838 at Carcoar, m Mary Ann Sheeler in 1858 at Mudgee, d 1917 at Hill End, buried at Tambaroora Cemetery

Matthew (U) – b 1843 at Penrith, m Mary Ann Hatch in 1862 in Albury, d 1918 at Tallangatta, buried at Albury Pioneer Cemetery. Notably first curator of the Albury Botanic Gardens. Note although Matthew died as Peasley, all of his children were born Peisley

Mary – b 1844 at Carcoar, m George Ridley in 1862 at Carcoar, d 1926 at Greenmantle or Crookwell, burial place unknown

William – b 1846 at Carcoar, m Mary Elvin in 1868 at Carcoar, d 1925 at Canowindra

Known children born with George Wilson

Ellen (Alley) – b 1849 at Carcoar

Agnes - b 1852 at Bathurst

George - b 1854 at Bathurst

Robert - b 1856 at Bathurst, died at birth

The Sydney Morning Herald.

VOL. XXIII.   TUESDAY, APRIL 18, 1848.   No. 3405

To the Editors of the Sydney Morning Herald.

GENTLEMEN,— As a lonely and desolate woman, deprived by the interference of the law of the aid and support of a husband, and unacquainted with the means of obtaining redress by an appeal to law, and unable, through poverty, to do so, I now take the liberty of soliciting a space in the columns of your very widely circulated journal, to present to the public notice a plain and simple statement of *facts* connected with the conviction of my husband, in the fond hope that it may meet the eyes either of His Excellency the Governor or some of the humane and influential members of the legal profession, and induce them to afford a due consideration to the case, and obtain for my husband not any extension of *clemency*, not any act of *mercy*, but to afford to an innocent man that *justice* to which he is entitled

The case is simply as follows:— In the month of January, 1846, my husband, Thomas Peisley, lost a young bull of the Durham breed, *unbranded*, which had been saved for a man named Thomas Pye, who had requested my husband to preserve one for him. After a long and fruitless search for the animal, my husband enquired of the poundkeeper, at Carcoar, whether a beast of the description had been ever noticed by him, or whether such an one had ever been sold from thence. The poundkeeper replied that one answering exactly to the description given was then in the pound, having been impounded from Mr. Icely's, by *John Kater*, the overseer of Mr. Icely. My husband recognised the beast as being his lost property, and on being informed by the poundkeeper that £5 damages had been laid, he declined paying anything but the poundage— saying that the overseer might sue him for the damage if he liked, for the bull was as good as any of Mr. Icely's. He then released the bull, took it home, and branded it. In some ten or twelve months afterwards, my husband was informed that John Kater, the same overseer for Mr. Icely, had taken the same bull, another bull, and other cattle, sending the other bull and other cattle to the pound, but detaining the bull before alluded to. My husband, on ascertaining that such was really the case, went himself to Kater and demanded by what authority he detained his (my husband's) beast. Kater replied that he detained it because Mr. Icely had lost a bull of the same description, and he suspected this to be the bull lost. My husband then enquired whether or not Mr. Icely's bull was branded, to which Kater replied in the affirmative, stating that it was branded TI on the hip and shoulder. My husband then told him that this bull could not be Mr. Icely's, as there was no other brand upon it but his own. Kater replied that he did not care, but that he would detain the beast until the arrival of Mr. Icely. My husband told him that it was optional with him whether he would leave it or not, but he left it until Mr. Icely's arrival, a period of about eight weeks. On Mr. Icely's arrival my husband, instead of obtaining his beast, was apprehended upon a warrant procured by Mr. Icely from his brother-in-law, Mr. Rotheray, upon Mr. Icely's farm, whither he had gone for the purpose of claiming his property. He was subsequently committed upon a charge of cattle stealing.

My husband was brought to trial at the Bathurst Assizes, February, 1848, on which occasion the following is an abstract of the evidence adduced:—

Mr. ICELY swore to the beast, and said that it was branded TI on the shoulder.

JOHN KATER swore to the same effect.

Mr. ROTHERAY swore to the same effect.

C. SPINKS, the Carcoar poundkeeper, swore to its being branded in the manner described by Messrs. Icely and Rotheray, though the *Gazette* was produced in Court in which this identical witness had published the same beast as *unbranded!*

MARK MILLS, Mr. Icely's stockman, deposed: That he himself brought in the bull in question, and took it to the pound by the order of John Kater, as a *strange* and *unbranded* beast, and laid thereon the damages of £5; he also swore to having seen Mr. Icely's bull two days previous to impounding the bull in question.

JAMES WILLIAMS, ticket-of-leave holder, deposed: That he was herdsman to Mr. Icely before Mills; that he roped and threw Mr. Icely's calf, and that Mr. J. Kinchela branded it. He had seen the calf scores of times since, and saw Mr. Icely's brand upon it; the last time he saw the calf it was eighteen months old; he then saw the brand quite plain. The witness was then sent from the box by the Attorney-General, and desired to examine the bull in question. On his return, the Attorney-General enquired whether the bull was branded? He replied that it was branded TP—TP. The Attorney-General enquired what other brand was on it? The witness replied—none. The Attorney-General enquired what brand was on the shoulder? The witness answered—No brand; nor any brand whatever on the cheek.

JOHN MOWAT: Was sixteen years in the service of Mr. Icely; was overseer over all his stock; in January, 1846, he was leaving Mr. Icely's service, and had to muster all his stock; at this muster he mustered Mr. Icely's bull, which was plainly branded TI *hip and shoulder*.

Such was the evidence upon which my husband was found *guilty*, and sentenced to be worked upon the roads for seven years.

I should here remark that upwards of two hundred individuals examined the bull during the course of the trial, none of whom could discern Mr. Icely's or any other brand than my husband's thereon.

As my husband was unable to afford to keep servants in his employment, and compelled, therefore, to look after his farm himself, he had no witnesses to adduce in his behalf; but the case, such as it is, is now submitted to the notice of the public. I submit it to their notice without comment, leaving it to themselves to draw the inference, whether *justice* has been done or not. I, however, humbly trust that my appeal to public sympathy may not be vain, and that the *God of the afflicted* will raise up for me and mine such friends as may support my humble claim for, and obtain for my oppressed husband that *justice* which a British subject is entitled to demand from the laws of his country.

ELIZABETH PEISLEY.
Little Forest, Carcoar,
April 4th, 1848.

Index

Albury Banner and Wodonga Express .... *See* Newspapers

Anti-Chinese Bill 61

Australian Police Gazette 37

Bathurst Assizes 27

Bathurst Free Press and Mining Journal .... *See* Newspapers

Bathurst Gaol .... *See* Gaols

Bathurst Times .... *See* Newspapers

Beardmore, Owen 63, 80, 87, 93, 122, 127, 154

Bell's Life in Sydney .... *See* Newspapers

Benyon, Martha 112, 136

Benyon, Stephen 112

Benyon, William 5, 98, 111, 121, 127, 131, 140, 153

Big Mouthed Scotchy 69

Bigga 75, 78, 86, 111, 123, 131

Binalong 65

Binda 124

Bullfrog, Jackie 41, 141, 147

Bushrangers
    Gardiner, Frank 7, 45, 73, 77, 84, 86, 93, 95, 101, 107, 112, 150
    Gilbert, John 152
    Hall, Ben 7, 96
    Kelly, Ned 7

Caloola 74

Carcoar .. 9, 14, 15, 27, 33, 63, 79, 93, 96, 127

Carcoar watch-house .... *See* Gaols

Certificate of Freedom 14

Clayton, Elizabeth. *See* Peisley, Elizabeth

Clayton, Matthew 23

Cockatoo Island .... *See* Gaols

Colonial Secretary 59

Colonial Treasurer 15

Conditional pardon 24
Cooming Park 9, 15, 19
Cosgrove, John 72
Cowper, Charles 52, 58
Darlinghurst Gaol .... See Gaols
Drady, John 98
Drady, Owen 9, 33
Durham bull 17
East, Henry 58
Empire .... See Newspapers
Escort Rock 152
Eugowra Gold Robbery 152
Eureka Rebellion 62
Fish River 75, 77, 102, 106, 107
Fitzroy Dock 50
Fogg, William 77, 84, 94, 97
Freeman's Journal .... See Newspapers
Gaols
    Bathurst Gaol 5, 36, 128, 139
    Carcoar watch-house 34
    Cockatoo Island 9, 21, 36, 45, 49, 55, 95, 111, 154
    Darlinghurst Gaol 21, 154
    Goulburn Gaol 98
    Gundagai Police lockup 132
    Old Bailey 23
    Parramatta Gaol 44, 45
    Pentridge Gaol 95
    Weatherboard 37, 45
Gardiner, Frank .... See Bushrangers
Gennys, John 82
Gilbert, John .... See Bushrangers
Golden Age (Queanbeyan) 129
Goulburn 124
Goulburn Herald .... See Newspapers

Green, Sarah 23
Grubbingbong 33
Gundagai Police lockup .... See Gaols
Gunning Flat 65
Hall, Ben .... See Bushrangers
Hanrigan, Johanna 66
Hill End 144
Hobbs, William 46
Holroyd, Arthur 19, 34, 71, 133
Hosie bribe 141
Hosie, William 63, 67, 71, 75, 77, 84, 86, 94, 101, 106, 108, 121, 127, 145, 149
Icely, Thomas 9, 15, 26, 82, 153
Invisible Prince 106
Jemalong 102
Kater, John 26
Kelly, Ned .... See Bushrangers
Kurley, Patrick 35
Lachlan Gold Escort 152
Lambing Flat 61, 80, 96, 97
Maitland Mercury .... See Newspapers
Marengo 103
Marsden, Reverend Samuel 13
McGuiness, Thomas 79, 97, 111, 134, 140
McKell, Thomas 34
Meyer, Solomon 82
Middleton 67
Middleton, John 63, 67, 77, 84, 93, 96, 121, 127, 145, 149
Mills, Mark 28
Morriss, Constable 124
Mountain Run Creek 72

164

Mowat, John 29
Mundarlo 126
New Police Regulation Act 149
New South Wales Police Gazette 66, 69, 102, 103
Newspapers
    Albury Banner and Wodonga Express 123, 125
    Bathurst Free Press and Mining Journal 34, 64, 70, 71, 72, 73, 74, 75, 81, 84, 105, 106, 108, 144
    Bathurst Times 68
    Bell's Life in Sydney 60, 144
    Empire 35, 47, 51, 55, 58, 93, 145
    Freeman's Journal 73
    Goulburn Herald 67, 109, 150
    Maitland Mercury 63
    South Australian Register 52
    Sydney Mail 104
    Sydney Morning Herald 3, 24, 30, 44, 68, 105
    Yass Courier 104, 150
North, Edward 82
Nowlan, Frederick 58
Old Bailey .... *See* Gaols
Orange 63, 69, 152
Ormsby, Charles 50, 52
Parkes, Henry 51
Parliamentary "Hulk Act" 12
Parramatta Gaol .... *See* Gaols
Peisley, Benjamin 6
Peisley, Elizabeth 6, 16, 23
Peisley, Thomas 11, 23, 25
Peisley's Creek 16
Pentridge Gaol .... *See* Gaols
Petitions 143

Pinacle 73
Police Act 62
Police Regulation Bill 62, 81
Pottinger, Frederick 63
Ridley, Mary Ann 99
Rockley 74
Rocky Bridge Creek 15
Samson, Mary Ann 135
Scone 60
South Australian Register .... *See* Newspapers
Sydney Benevolent Asylum 24
Sydney Mail .... *See* Newspapers
Sydney Morning Herald *See* Newspapers
Tambaroora 68, 144
Tarcutta 124
Taylor, Adam 97
Taylor, James 98
Taylor, Mary Annetta 97
Taylor, Richard 98
Taylor, Sophia 97
Taylor, William 98
The Argus 123
Thunderbolt, Captain 55
Ticket of Leave 21, 45, 47
Tuena 63, 66, 77, 108, 122
Vane, John 99
Walsh, Bridget "Biddy" 98
Walsh, Catherine "Kitty" 98
Walsh, Michael 70
Ward, Frederick 55
Watt, John 70

Weatherboard............................*See* Gaols
Weavers, Thomas 35
Williams, James 28
Wilson, George 30
Wilson, James 111
Wilson, Jane 136
Windeyer, WIlliam 39
Wylie, George 46
Yass 21, 103
Yass Courier.................... *See* Newspapers
Young... 61

www.ingramcontent.com/pod-product-compliance
Lightning Source LLC
Chambersburg PA
CBHW062036290426
44109CB00026B/2640